LONDON SW1

3 30 PM
6 FEB
1952

1 1/2 d POSTAGE 1 1/2 d
2' REVENUE 2'

QUEEN ELIZABETH II

A Portrait in Stamps

FAY SWEET

Royal Mail

THE BRITISH LIBRARY

Contents

CHANGING FACES

When Antony Williams' portrait of the Queen was unveiled in the late 1990s it met with rare approval. The large painting shows the Queen seated and gazing into the distance. She is portrayed with little royal adornment – her only jewellery is a modest bracelet. There is absolutely no ostentation. We are shown the 70-year-old monarch dignified, but looking her age, and even slightly careworn. How human and how different in style from royal portraits of the past. Even the fact that it is painted in the flat finish of tempera rather than in the more traditional glossy oil marks the vast change that has occurred in royal portraiture over the centuries.

Portraits have always played a vitally important role in our perception of the monarchy. There can be no more imposing image of English royalty than that of broad-shouldered Henry VIII, resplendent in his most elaborate garb. His familiar portrait – by an artist from the circle of Hans Holbein the Younger – is an expression of confidence and authority, a depiction of the fearless king who took on the might of the Pope and the Church, leaving an indelible mark on British history. Of course, the art of portraiture existed long before Henry VIII, but it was during his reign that it acquired new import. The portrait retained its role as a record of the rich and powerful, a gift and a keepsake, but with Henry's break from Rome it also became a propaganda tool; Henry was more than a mere mortal – he was god-like. Positive imagery was essential for a king who had taken on established powers and who needed loyal support to win the day.

A gallery of kings and queens on stamps, by unknown 16th-century artists and present-day photographer Lord Snowdon (opposite)

Henry's daughter Elizabeth I proved to be highly adept at image control too. In her early portraits she appears as a pious, demure girl – perfect for sending to a prospective suitor. However, as her long reign progressed, her image became highly stylised. As Elizabeth continued her father's quarrel with Rome, she knew it was imperative to depict herself in paintings laden with celestial symbols to reinforce the idea of monarchy as a god-given right. The astute Elizabeth even introduced laws to control how she was portrayed, and approved images were made available for copying. Unflattering portraits were tracked down and burned. English painter Nicholas Hilliard, famed for his miniatures, recorded that Elizabeth I insisted on being painted out of doors, in full sunlight 'where no tree was neere, nor any shadow at all'.

ARTIST UNKNOWN c.1575 / HARRISON

The apotheosis of this era was reached in the famous Ditchley Portrait by Marcus Gheerhaerts the Younger. Painted when the Queen was in her late 60s, the figure portrayed is a virgin-white, translucent, celestial being – Gloriana. The uppermost parts of her body are placed in the heavens while her feet are planted firmly in Oxfordshire.

As a clear indication of how times have changed – and that we now accept the monarchy as mortal – our own royal family has allowed its members to be shown in ways which would surely have sent a shudder down Tudor spines. The modern style makes a much less intimidating monarchy – the Queen and Prince Philip smile warmly back at us.

Our changing perceptions of the monarchy are inextricably linked to the dawning of the age of mass media. And since the current royal family is the first to be fully exposed to the invention of the camera, it has undergone

unprecedented scrutiny. Nevertheless we are still moved by the monarchy with all its symbolism and pageantry. Despite the gulf between populace and monarch being almost closed, the sovereign's portrait continues to stand as a powerful national icon, not least on coins and banknotes and, of course, postage stamps.

Here, within the pages of this book, the story of our Queen's reign is told in stamps. These are stamps which chart the important events and national preoccupations of the past half century, which capture the mood of the times and also provide an invaluable and intriguing record of the evolution of modern royal portraiture. As miniature works of art and powerful ambassadors for Britain, these stamps have travelled the globe in their billions and have ensured that the Queen's portrait is not only one of the most familiar in the modern world, but arguably the most reproduced image of all time.

When Sir Rowland Hill introduced the Penny Black in 1840, he set the archetypal standard for British stamps. As the country which invented the postage stamp, the UK  is the only nation not to include its full country name on its stamps; instead, the nation is signified by the face of the reigning monarch. The features of the individual become an instantly-recognizable icon of the country of origin. By convention, the monarch's face always looks to his or her right on the 'everyday' small-format definitive stamps. Royal Mail uses an exacting system of design commissioning, consultation and proofing to produce its stamps, but the final say lies with Her Majesty. All stamp designs are presented to the Queen and all must receive royal approval before they can be issued.

A New
Elizabethan Era

1950s

‘By the sudden death of my dear father I am called to assume the duties and responsibility of sovereignty. My heart is too full for me to say more to you today than that I shall always work, as my father did throughout his reign, to uphold constitutional government and to advance the happiness and prosperity of my peoples, spread as they are the world over.’

THE DECLARATION
OF ACCESSION,
FEBRUARY 1952

TIMELINE

1952
Death of King George VI (6 February)
Queen Elizabeth's Accession Declaration
Funeral of King George VI at Windsor
The Queen's first State Opening of Parliament

1953
Coronation of Queen Elizabeth II (2 June)
Arrival in New Zealand the Queen and the Duke of
  Edinburgh at the start of Commonwealth Tour

1954
Arrival in Australia of the Queen and Duke
  of Edinburgh
Return to UK after Commonwealth Tour

1955
Sir Winston and Lady Churchill welcome the Queen
  and Duke of Edinburgh to 10 Downing Street to
  attend Sir Winston's retirement dinner (4 April)
State visit to Norway

1956
Queen's tour of Nigeria
State visit with the Duke of Edinburgh to Sweden
Received state visit from King Feisal of Iraq

1957
State visits to Portugal, France and Denmark
Visit to Canada and United States. In October the
  Queen opened the 23rd Canadian Parliament,
  the first Sovereign to open the Canadian Parliament
  in person. The Queen addresses a special meeting
  of the United Nations General Assembly in New York

1958
State visit to the Netherlands
Received state visit from President Gronchi of Italy
Received state visit from President Heuss of Germany

1959
Tour of Canada and visit to the United States
Received state visit from the Shahanshah of Iran
Announced that Queen expecting a baby

The 1950s were some of the toughest years of the century in Britain. When George VI died in 1952, the 25-year-old Princess Elizabeth became Queen of a nation that was still impoverished, bomb-shattered and emotionally drained by the War. Though it had ended in 1945, the Second World War had lasted far longer than anyone had expected – and victory had been won at a high price. The country found itself with appalling shortages of houses, coal and food.

Rebuilding the nation was an incredibly difficult task and while the 1951 Festival of Britain provided a welcome splash of colour and entertainment, the rationing and hardship continued for years. As the major nations re-aligned, the threat of nuclear conflict cast its long shadow over the 1950s. Real war was replaced by a Cold War (the UK exploded its first atomic bomb in the accession year).

Nevertheless, the Coronation was an occasion of great national jubilation in 1953, and gradually the future started to look brighter as austerity gave way to increasing affluence.

By the end of the decade the United Kingdom had lost ground as a world power (the Suez crisis and the dismantling of the Empire took care of that) but Prime Minister Harold Macmillan was telling the British people that they had 'never had it so good'. Though the structure of society and the Establishment in Britain looked much as it had done before the War (with the monarchy in particular enjoying great popularity) the 1950s saw the first stirrings of rebellion and the questioning of the old order. The 'Angry Young Men' of British theatre were determined to crash through what they saw as the hypocritical politeness of middle-class life and confront audiences with the realities, pain and humour of the working classes. Teenagers, meanwhile, looked to America where Elvis was rockin' and rollin' with shocking success. Britain responded by producing some luminous home-grown stars – Tommy Steele, Cliff Richard and Diana Dors. It was the age of Pop Art, Cool Jazz, The Goons and, as Queen Elizabeth acknowledged when she allowed her Christmas speech to be televised for the first time in 1958, it was the age of television.

GOD SAVE THE QUEEN

On the chill morning of 6 February 1952, the British people were stunned as news spread of the sudden death of their much-loved King George VI, aged just 56. His successor, Princess Elizabeth, was taking part in a royal tour of East Africa with her husband when she heard the news and immediately cut short the visit to return home as Queen. As she stepped from a BOAC aircraft at London Airport she was met by Prime Minister Winston Churchill and other politicians to face the affairs of state.

At the Accession Council on 8 February, the young 25-year-old Queen (the same age as Elizabeth I was when she took the throne) made her accession declaration. She pledged 'that I shall always work, as my father did throughout his reign, to uphold constitutional government and to advance the happiness and prosperity of my peoples, spread as they are the world over'. The accession was publicly proclaimed throughout the UK and much of the Commonwealth

The new Queen arrives home from Kenya

that day, in the first occasion of pageantry of the Queen's reign. This was a brief note of rejoicing amid the mourning of the King. By old custom, flags were run up to their full height for a few hours after the proclamation.

The new Elizabethan age had dawned, its tone set by a young glamorous Queen, her husband, the Duke of Edinburgh, and their two young children Charles and Anne.

Court mourning officially came to an end in June 1952, and the coronation was set for 2 June 1953. There followed a year of royal firsts for the Queen: investitures, official visits, the state opening of Parliament and on Christmas Day 1952 the Queen made the first Christmas broadcast of her reign from the study at Sandringham, using the chair and desk that had served King George VI and before him King George V for the same purpose. Her words were addressed to all peoples of the Commonwealth and Empire and she promised to strive

to continue the work of her father and grandfather to unite the members of that family ever more closely. She also asked her subjects to pray for her on her Coronation Day.

The crowning of Elizabeth II, like any prestigious national event, required lengthy and detailed planning. Even though there were 16 months between accession and coronation, there were literally thousands of items to be considered. A Coronation Commission was established as early as April 1952, and committees were soon establishing designs for souvenirs, commemorative medals, emblems and pageantry, as well as the weightier task of organizing the attendance of heads of states, the procession route and preparations in Westminster Abbey. High-profile commissions included weaving the purple velvet for the coronation robe.

The coronation was a break in the clouds of austerity for British people. At long last wartime rationing was easing. Hundreds of thousands of people, many of whom had camped out overnight to secure the best views, braved the cold and rain to see the gold State Coach pass by – used for every coronation since George IV. Some 20 million people are estimated to have watched the ceremony live on TV. It was the Queen who insisted, against the wishes of her Cabinet, that the coronation be televised so that as many people as possible could observe the ancient ceremony, culminating in the crowning of the monarch by the Archbishop of Canterbury. The St Edward's Crown (incidentally, the crown borne on Royal Mail's logo) is worn by the sovereign on this one occasion only, and was created for Charles II's investiture. As the icing on the cake, on Coronation Day news reached the UK that Mount Everest had been conquered by Edmund Hillary and Tenzing Norgay. It seemed symbolic of the dawning of a new era. As the Queen noted in her coronation broadcast that evening: 'I am sure that this, my coronation, is not a symbol of power and a splendour that are gone but a

ABOVE **The Queen gives her first Christmas message, 1952**

LEFT AND BELOW **Souvenir programmes from the coronation**

A Dorothy Wilding
portrait of the Queen
from the sessions which
produced the image for
the first stamps of
her reign

declaration of our hopes for the future and for the years I may, by God's grace and mercy, be given to reign and serve as your Queen.'

Naturally, with the arrival of a new monarch there must be new issues of coins and stamps bearing the sovereign's head. Shortly after the accession, the Royal Mint set to work on a range of coinage featuring a sculpture by Mary Gillick. Meanwhile, designs for new stamps were progressing. The process began with the General Post Office (GPO) commissioning noted society photographer Dorothy Wilding to capture a suitable image of the Queen. During two photographic sessions many approaches were tried. Wilding experimented with different angles and backgrounds, some images featuring the Queen with a small crown, others with no crown at all. Finally a three-quarter profile of the Queen wearing the diadem was selected as the definitive portrait – which would remain in use for 15 years. At the same time the GPO and Council of

Industrial Design drew up a list of some 20 artists who were invited to submit ideas for new stamp designs. Their task was to frame the Wilding portrait with an appropriate border depicting the floral emblems of England, Scotland, Wales and Northern Ireland and incorporate the words 'Postage Revenue', together with the stamp's value.

From an original 75 designs, nine were selected to show the Queen – a quartet by Enid Marx, M.C. Farrar-Bell, Mary Adshead and Edmund Dulac were particularly recommended. The Queen approved this choice and also requested the addition of a fifth design by George Knipe, who had designed the 2½d Silver Wedding stamp for George VI and Queen Elizabeth four years earlier. The first

A range of definitive stamp designs featuring the Wilding portrait – the two on the left were the first two to be issued

RIGHT **One of Cecil Beaton's official coronation portraits**

BELOW **Commonwealth tributes to the coronation on subsequent anniversaries**

OPPOSITE **The approved proofs of the coronation stamps**

two stamps of the definitive series – those designed by Enid Marx and M.C. Farrar-Bell – were issued in December 1952; the subsequent 15 values were released between then and 1954.

With this work under way, attention turned to producing stamps to mark the coronation – the first commemorative issue of Elizabeth's reign. On this occasion 27 artists were asked to submit designs. In September 1952, meetings were held at GPO Headquarters in London to review the material and the work of four designers, Farrar-Bell, Edgar G. Fuller, Michael Goaman and Edmund Dulac. Tellingly, the art critic and historian Sir Kenneth Clark, after reviewing the work, recommended that portraits of Elizabeth I by Nicholas Hilliard be borne in mind when considering the image of the monarch for the new stamps. In the event, the portrait by Dorothy Wilding formed the centrepiece in most designs. The exception was that of Dulac's, for the 1/3d value, which featured his own splendid illustration of the Queen facing directly out of the stamp, perhaps capturing the nation's fairy-tale mood. The press reaction of the day,

8696

511

1483

399

*Final stamps approved for
design and colour.*

[signature]

31st March 1953

Dorothy Wilding was a celebrated society photographer who had enjoyed a long-standing relationship with the royal family; she had been capturing them on camera since the 1920s and took the first official photograph of the 11-year-old Princess Elizabeth. Wilding's work had already appeared on commemorative and Commonwealth stamps – her portraits of George VI and Queen Elizabeth were featured on the 1937 coronation stamp and the elegant silver wedding stamps of 1948. This combination of royal favour and philatelic experience made her the prime candidate for photographer of the portrait for the new definitive stamps.

Short, bespectacled and eccentric, Wilding had a reputation for establishing an easy rapport with her sitters. Her photographs of the glitterati of the day – from Noel Coward and Maurice Chevalier in the 1930s to Yul Brynner and Harry Belafonte in the 1950s – were immensely popular, and have a classic, timeless quality.

however, was not united in praise. 'The face is not entirely a happy piece of work – the Queen's mouth is too big', commented the *Manchester Guardian*. Sadly, Dulac died just days before his stamp design was issued. The four stamps were published on the day after the coronation.

QUEEN AND COMMONWEALTH

Britain's shifting place in the world during the past half century has been reflected in stamps and their design. No longer the headquarters of a worldwide Empire, in the 1950s Britain settled down to leading a commonwealth of nations. On her accession Queen Elizabeth II was billed as a rather different sort of monarch than her predecessors. The proclamation which began her reign was carefully worded to emphasise Britain's shrinking responsibilities as an imperial power. Indeed, her full statutory title at the time should have been: 'Elizabeth II by the Grace of God of Great Britain, Ireland and the British Dominions beyond the Seas, Queen, Defender of the Faith'. But this title was clearly out of date in several ways, not least the references to Ireland and to the newly or nearly independent nations as 'dominions' which would have wrongly implied subservience to Britain. Instead the old imperial vocabulary was replaced with

Royal visits commemorated in Commonwealth stamps of 1954 and 1957

a reference to the Queen as 'Head of the Commonwealth'. Over the next year and a half consultations took place with the Commonwealth governments of the day – both the monarchies of Canada, Australia, New Zealand and South Africa (which was to leave the Commonwealth in 1961) and the independent republics of India and Pakistan. Each country agreed a new title for the Queen, reflecting the change in her status, and a royal proclamation was issued throughout the Commonwealth, four days ahead of the coronation.

The Commonwealth was a powerful idea. In a 1952 broadcast Winston Churchill had avowed that the new monarch was 'the magic link which unites our loosely bound but strongly interwoven Commonwealth' and he added, perhaps a little optimistically, that 'famous have been the reigns of our Queens – some of the greatest periods of our history have unfolded under their sceptre'.

Her coronation behind her, the Queen determined to visit as many countries of the Commonwealth as could be sandwiched into six months of non-stop travel. Her 50,000 mile round-the-world itinerary still ranks as the longest royal tour ever. In the course of it she opened seven parliaments, attended 223 balls, banquets and receptions and made 157 speeches.

A young and glamorous figure, the Queen attracted vast crowds. In Australia, where she spent almost two months, three-quarters of the population managed to see her in person.

'Omnibus' designs for coronation stamps, which were used by several Commonwealth countries

DEPICTING THE COMMONWEALTH

By 1970, when the ninth British Commonwealth Games were held in Edinburgh, the regalia of the earlier stamps was replaced by images that gave centre stage to the athletes themselves. The stamps celebrated the movement of the runners, swimmers and cyclists featured on the three stamps, and also acknowledged that the competitors were from many ethnic groups.

By 1986 – again in Edinburgh – 'British' had been dropped from the title of the Games and, in the commemorative stamp issue, the 17 pence stamp showed a black athlete on his marks. 1965 had already seen a stamp set for the Commonwealth Arts Festival which acknowledged the legitimacy of indigenous arts by depicting Trinidad Carnival and Canadian Folk dancers. These stamps tied in neatly with royal tours – in 1964 the Queen had attended Canada's centennial celebrations and soon after the stamps were issued she embarked on a Caribbean tour.

Stamps reflected political changes, too. A special stamp was issued for the 1977 Commonwealth Heads of Government meeting. It represents the 'Gathering of Nations' and adopts a fastidiously diplomatic geometric design in which, literally, all sides are equal. Britain is one among many nations, sitting in the circle, not at the head of the table. In 1999, for the reflective Millennium series, the colonist Captain Cook is presented in a non-triumphalist way and given equal prominence with a New Zealand Maori. The Settlers Tale stamps from the same year give a similarly modern account of the colonial enterprise.

CASTLES OF THE REALM

A quartet of imposing castles drawn from the four corners of the realm were chosen as fitting symbols for the first high-value stamps of Queen Elizabeth's reign. It is difficult for us to imagine today, but in the 1950s this pictorial approach was an unusual one. Where stamps traditionally featured the monarch's head set in a decorative frame and perhaps alongside the royal coat of arms, the inclusion of a picture marked a significant change. In fact, there was a precedent. During George VI's reign a set of high-value stamps featured images of HMS *Victory*, the White Cliffs of Dover and St George and the Dragon. For the new monarch the artist Lynton Lamb produced exquisite paintings of the castles of Carrickfergus, Caernarfon, Edinburgh and Windsor (right). Each magnificent building was set in the same handsome rustic stone frame beside which was the Queen's portrait as photographed by the Wilding studio for the

standard definitives. Interestingly, it was this very same quartet of castles which became the subject of a subsequent series of high-value definitives in 1988. This time the images – based on photographs by Prince Andrew – show sections of the buildings used boldly to fill up the entire stamp frame, leaving just enough space for a silhouette of the Queen's head. In 1999 the castles series was eventually replaced with high-value definitives matching the

design of the lower-value stamps. The 1955 castles series had a rebirth when, for their fiftieth birthday, they were reissued all together in a miniature sheet, with revised values. Enormously popular with collectors, they were printed in the specialist intaglio process.

CAERNARFON CASTLE

ABOVE **1958 British Empire and Commonwealth Games commemorative stamps designed by (top to bottom): Reynolds Stone, W.H. Brown and P. Keely**

OPPOSITE **A ground-breaking informal image of the royal family by Lord Snowdon**

The popularity of the monarch and the regalia of her tour across the globe might have given the impression that the Empire was still intact, but the changing relationship between Britain and her former colonies was real and profoundly important. The shift was reflected in stamp issues across the Queen's reign. In 1958 the sporting event that everyone now knows simply as the Commonwealth Games was still, in this transitional period, called the British Empire and Commonwealth Games. The sixth games were held in Cardiff and the Queen used the event as an opportunity to announce that Prince Charles was to be created Prince of Wales. The three stamps that were issued to mark the occasion included one designed by Reynolds Stone, and were traditional in their design with a heavy emphasis on the symbolic Welsh Dragon and on banners and flags. A short decade later such a narrowly defined treatment would be unthinkable. Attitudes to the Commonwealth and the stamps which marked its milestone events had changed for ever.

Attitudes closer to home were also changing. The Queen's indications early on in her reign that she intended to make the monarchy more accessible became clearer at the end of the 1950s. Some traditions and customs were seen to have outlived their purpose or were out of step with the times. The 'presentation parties' for debutantes and traditional garden parties ended. A new style of garden party was introduced – at both Buckingham Palace and Holyroodhouse – to which a much broader cross-section of people were invited. Of the 40,000 people who attend each year, the majority come for the first time. Palace luncheons were instituted in 1956, enabling the Queen and Prince Philip to meet achievers in the arts, business, sport and public life. The education of her children was another area where royal tradition would be broken: the Queen and Prince Philip eschewed the system of personal tutors used for previous generations of royal children. But it was during the 1960s that some of the greatest changes occurred to society, royalty and, indeed, British stamps.

White Heat
of Technology

1960s

1st

> ❝In the Commonwealth we start with the advantage of sharing many ways of looking at things and doing things. This makes co-operation between our countries easier, but our Governments will, in the long run, only be as close as their people feel.❞

FIRST COMMONWEALTH DAY
MESSAGE, MAY 1965

TIMELINE

1960
Birth of Prince Andrew (19 February)
Received state visits from President de Gaulle
of France, King Bhumibol of Thailand,
King Mahendra of Nepal
Queen restores surname of Mountbatten to the
family name. Henceforth descendants would
be Mountbatten-Windsors
Marriage of Princess Margaret to
Lord Snowdon

1961
State visits to Cyprus, India, Pakistan, Nepal,
Iran and Turkey, followed by visits to Italy and
the Vatican.
Visits to Ghana, Sierra Leone, the Gambia
and Liberia

1962
Prince Charles begins his first term
at Gordonstoun
The Queen attended the consecration of the new
Coventry Cathedral
Visit to the Netherlands to attend celebrations
of silver wedding anniversary of Queen Juliana
and Prince Bernhard
Received state visit from President Tubman of
Liberia and King Olav V of Norway

1963
Tour of New Zealand and Australia, visiting
Fiji en route
Received state visits from King Baudouin of
Belgium, President Radhakrishan of India and
King Paul I of Greece

1964
Visit to Canada for centennial celebrations
Birth of Prince Edward (10 March)
Received state visit from President Ferik Ibrahim
Abbood of Sudan

1965
State visits to Ethiopia and Sudan, and Federal
Republic of Germany, including a visit
to Berlin
Received state visit from President de Frei
of Chile
The Queen led celebrations for the 700th
anniversary of Simon de Montfort's
Parliament and the 900th anniversary of
Westminster Abbey
State funeral of Winston Churchill
Opening of Post Office Tower

1966
Queen's Caribbean tour
State visit to Belgium
Received state visits from President Jonas of
Austria, King Hussein of Jordan, President
Ayub Khan of Pakistan

1967
State visit to Canada for 100th anniversary of
Confederation and visit to Expo 67
Visit to Malta – first state visit as Sovereign to
an independent Malta
Received state visits from King Faisal of Saudi
Arabia and President Cevdet Sunay of Turkey

1968
State visits to Chile and Brazil
Prince Andrew starts his first term at prep school

1969
State visit to Austria
Prince Charles invested as Prince of Wales
at Caernarfon Castle (July 1)
Royal Family TV film
Received state visits from President Saragat of
Italy and President Kekkonen of Finland

THE 1960s

The decade which followed the austere, monochrome 1950s was, by contrast, a technicolour era of confidence and consumer spending. In the Swinging Sixties the skirts were short and London became the fashion capital of the world. The older generation was alarmed at what they saw as the collapse of personal morality and discipline. For others it was just a great time to be young. The Beatles, who had made their debut at the Cavern Club in Liverpool in 1961, became the most famous pop group in the world. Fans gathered at Buckingham Palace when they received their MBEs from the Queen in 1965. It was the decade of scandal and satire, of the Krays and the Moors Murders. England won the World Cup and James Bond became the glamorous personification of British cool.

Internationally it was a time of assassinations. President Kennedy, his brother Robert and the civil rights leader Martin Luther King were murdered. China declared a cultural revolution and America went to war in Vietnam. Russian tanks rolled into Prague. Despite the Cold War and nuclear brinkmanship, Britain was in an expansive mood. The consecration of the new Coventry Cathedral, attended by the Queen, seemed symbolic of how a better, modern world could rise from the ashes of the old.

The death of Churchill in the mid-1960s marked the end of an era. Now Britons put their faith in what the Labour Prime Minister Harold Wilson famously referred to as 'the white heat of technology'. Rebuilding in Britain touched every part of the country – from the Forth Road Bridge to London Underground's new Victoria Line – which were both opened by the Queen. The Sixties witnessed the acceleration of man into space. What had begun with Yuri Gagarin's first ever manned orbit of the globe in 1961, culminated in the arrival of the first man on the moon in 1969.

THE BIRTH OF SPECIAL STAMPS

On the surface, the 1950s and early 1960s were years of economic expansion and prosperity. Since the mid-1950s the economic well-being of the average Briton rose dramatically and visibly, despite regular cycles of inflation. In this period, however, Britain's share of world trade fell with almost perfect consistency by about one per cent a year. The economic concern of government was to increase productivity and ensure labour peace so that Britain could again become an exporting nation. National Productivity Year was therefore celebrated with a commemorative stamp issue in 1962 and the spirit of industry and technological endeavour in the Wilson years, from 1964, spilled over into every area of life. The modernising tendency extended further into the stamps programme where there was pressure from designers to liberalise stamp policy – especially with regard to pictorial, commemorative stamps.

There was nothing new about commemoratives. The first UK stamp to mark an occasion, rather than an 'everyday' definitive stamp, was issued for the British Empire Exhibition in 1924, and they were periodically released for major events and royal and postal occasions. In the early 1960s, the scope of these stamps was widened and gradually more were issued each year. With the new Labour administration came refined criteria for the issuing of the 'Special Stamps' which remain to this day. Stamps were to be issued to: commemorate important anniversaries, celebrate events of importance, reflect the British contribution to world affairs, reflect the British way of life, and extend public patronage of the arts by encouraging design.

At this time, designers were invited to submit ideas they might have on the future development of design policy and, in response, the artist David Gentleman submitted a long memorandum. Gentleman had already been successful in having his stamp designs accepted, but he took the view that better, more daring design standards could only be achieved if an alternative element to the Wilding photographic portrait of the Queen could be found. He was

BELOW **National Productivity Year stamps, 1962, by David Gentleman**

RIGHT **The first UK commemorative stamp, issued in 1924**

commissioned to prepare an 'album' of alternative stamp designs – including some quite radical proposals without the image of the monarch – which showed what was possible if the designer had a free hand.

In the Wilson administration, Anthony Wedgwood Benn had been given the job of Postmaster General. Benn spoke of stamps as 'part of the arts' and was interested in the messages they could send abroad about progressive Britain. He determined to go to the Queen and gauge her reaction to stamp designs that did not carry the monarch's head.

In his diary Benn recalls the moment in 1965 when, during an audience at Buckingham Palace, he spread the designs and the Gentleman album on the floor at the Queen's feet: 'I knelt on the floor and one after another passed up to the Queen the Battle of Britain stamps bearing the words 'Great Britain' but no royal head. It was a most hilarious scene because I had all my papers all over the place and she was peering at something that obviously had never been shown to her or even thought about at the Palace before.' Although the Queen was charming, change took a little longer.

When David Gentleman's stamps marking the 25th anniversary of the Battle of Britain were issued in September 1965 they were controversial – but not because the Queen's head was missing. They caused a row because one of the six stamps showed the wreck of a Dornier German bomber with a swastika clearly visible on the fin. Although the aeroplane was portrayed as half-submerged in water, the image offended some people and questions were asked in Parliament.

ABOVE **Tony Benn as new Postmaster General, 1964**

BELOW **Alternative Gentleman designs without the monarch's head**

Battle of Britain 1940

4d

4d Welsh mountains /autumn

Sussex coast

4d

Meanwhile David Gentleman spent a year experimenting with royal cyphers and coats of arms, all in silhouette, which could be used on stamps. Eventually a solution was found and he settled on a silhouette head of the Queen, based on the profile which appeared on the coinage. The landscape series of stamps issued in 1966 became the first stamps to use this image of the Queen, albeit at quite a dominating proportion.

Sussex   ENGLAND   4d
L ROSOMAN   HARRISON AND SONS LTD

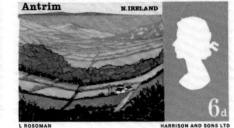

Antrim   N. IRELAND   6d
L ROSOMAN   HARRISON AND SONS LTD

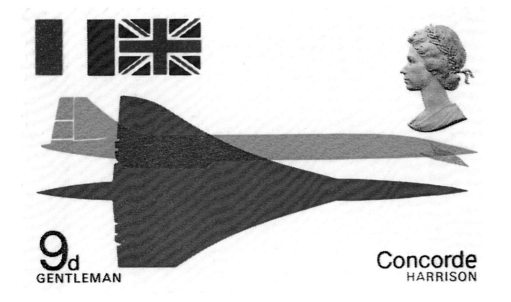

9d
GENTLEMAN

Concorde
HARRISON

Gentleman's labours set the tone for stamp design for the next 20 years. To see the change in progress, it is interesting to compare the approach of the first Gentleman-designed stamps from 1962 commemorating National Productivity Year with the much more graphically diverse and colourful stamps which marked British Technology in 1966 (Benn had became Technology Minister that year) and the First Flight of Concorde in 1969.

FORTH ROAD BRIDGE

Standing as a remarkable tribute to British engineering expertise, the Forth Road Bridge was opened by the Queen on 4 September 1964. It immediately hit the record books as Europe's longest suspension bridge at one and a half miles (1.8km) long. This 'Highway to the Sky' was the pride of Scotland, spanning the Firth of Forth between North and South Queensferry and making a fast road link between Edinburgh and Dunfermline. The bridge replaced the regular ferry which had been in service for a full 800 years.

Standing alongside the Forth Rail Bridge (opened in 1890 by the Prince of Wales) the newer, elegant structure remains distinguished by its twin towers, each over 500 feet (150m) high, and the great arch of its four-lane roadway – all held in place with seven thousand feet of steel cable.

Sitting side by side, the rail and road bridges provide a startling comparison of the engineering feats of two different centuries. The pair of commemorative stamps was designed by Andrew Restall; one depicts the new bridge as a bold graphic image, the other shows the pair of bridges side by side. Both stand as fine examples of contemporary graphic design.

THE QUEEN AND THE COMMONERS

The Wilson administration looked upon the honours list to reward more people in vocations previously overlooked or not recognized to a great extent, such as actors, sportspeople, journalists and social workers. The awarding

Festival. Gentleman placed England's most illustrious playwright and commoner across the stage, as it were, from the portrait of the Queen with stylised characters from the plays separating them. Later, the very powerful and large

of the MBE to each of the four Beatles created a storm of protests, and nine people sent their decorations back to the Palace. A common complaint was: 'Churchill would never have done this!' But more controversy was to arise from the honour of being depicted on a Special Stamp.

image of Churchill which appeared on commemorative stamps after his death in 1965 tipped the balance still further, although in most cases people other than the Queen represented on stamps were anonymous, such as the footballers jostling on the 1966 World Cup stamps.

Before the revolution in stamp design in the mid-1960s, when the photographic portrait of the Queen was replaced with an elegant silhouette, there had been a debate about whether it was appropriate for the monarch to be shown alongside a commoner on a stamp. The first time this happened was in 1964 on David Gentleman's stamp designs commemorating the 400th anniversary of Shakespeare's birth and the Shakespeare

But it was in that year, when the Queen appeared on a stamp with the Scottish poet Robert Burns, that there was real disquiet. After all, hadn't Burns been a dissolute drinker whose life was complicated by his many love affairs? But then this was the 1960s – the spirit of the times was more about tolerance and equality than disapproval – and this was reflected in stamps.

THE QUEEN AND HER PRIME MINISTERS

Unlike Disraeli's perceived policy of 'flattering' Queen Victoria, Queen Elizabeth II has enjoyed a remarkably close relationship with her 11 Prime Ministers. At the weekly meetings at Buckingham Palace she is briefed on government issues, but she is also a source of rich experience and advice that PMs have come to rely on. Winston Churchill, her first Prime Minister, was particularly

impressed with the Queen. The feeling was evidently mutual: the Queen broke with precedent and was the first sovereign to attend the State funeral of one of her subjects when Churchill died in 1965 (left). The stamp issue to honour Churchill was the first to commemorate a contemporary individual. He was to be featured again forty years later in a stamp issue on the National Portrait Gallery in 2006.

Prime Ministers' memoirs frequently refer to the Queen's sound advice, especially on foreign and diplomatic questions. The language of these memoirs often reveals a real respect and admiration for the Queen. Her Majesty can also serve as an informal non-political support to the Prime Minister. The Royal Prerogative in fact enabled the Queen to choose the next Prime Minister without advice. However, by the mid 1960s, the leading political parties had changed the way they elected their leaders and the scope of the Prerogative was greatly reduced.

MACHIN AND THE MODERN IMAGE

Stamp imagery and other portraits of the Queen provide a snapshot of attitudes to the Crown in terms of what is perceived as appropriate iconography for the times, as well as conveying their public image and reputation. The rise in public visibility of the Royal Family since the 1960s is mirrored in these images. At the beginning of the decade, as the young Queen's family grew, relatively informal portraits of her with her youngest children portrayed an air of domesticity. The 1969 painting of the Queen by Pietro Annigoni, in contrast, is a deeply romanticised portrait, with the Queen standing alone, cloaked in ceremonial robes against a cloudless sky, and suggestive of the loneliness of monarchy. When unveiled in February 1970, the *Evening News* went so far as to sympathize with the Queen: 'In (the) new portrait, unveiled today at the National Portrait Gallery, all the joy seems to have gone. Those eyes once sparkling, are worried and sad with a tearful hint of a red rim'. As ever, the public were the final judge, and an astonishing 200,000 people went to see the portrait in the first month.

A sensitive image by Cecil Beaton of the Queen with baby Prince Edward and young Prince Andrew in 1964

As with formal portraits, so with the official iconography of the definitive stamps. When artist Arnold Machin set to work on his exquisite sculpted portrait of the Queen, he could have had little idea that this timeless design would become the world's most reproduced image. It is estimated that it has been printed more than 175 billion times. The familiar portrait, seen the world over, has remained in constant, daily use for more than four decades.

The stamp design evolved to replace the Wilding definitives which had put in sterling service since 1952, the year of the Queen's accession. However, by the 1960s the first definitive series was in need of updating and refreshing. Britain's art and design scene was one of the most exciting and forward-looking in the world, and new stamps would provide an important reflection of the changing times.

The first steps towards creating a new design were taken in the mid-1960s when Postmaster General Tony Benn obtained the Queen's permission to prepare studies for a new definitive series. The GPO commissioned stamp printers and a number of designers to produce ideas for alternative portraits to the Wilding photograph. Part of the brief was also to show how the new portrait might be incorporated into definitive and special issue designs. One of those approached was Arnold Machin, artist and Master of Sculpture at the Royal Academy School.

Machin was at the time working on a new portrait for the first range of decimal coins which would appear in 1968. The bas-relief concept he produced for the coins was also used for the stamps, and Machin made a series of several sculptures with different approaches. When the submissions from all designers were shown to the Stamp Advisory Committee, it was Machin's concept which gained most favour. The portrait was contemporary and elegant and yet also showed its shared heritage with the Penny Black. Machin's own explanation for the design's popularity was simple: 'Because it [the Queen's head] wasn't a photograph, it was more acceptable as a symbol and could survive without looking ridiculous.'

With the committee's approval, Machin worked further on refining his design. In the first and second casts, the Queen was portrayed wearing a small tiara. However, in the third and final design she was shown in the diadem also seen in the Wilding portrait. By the autumn of 1966 the designs were ready to put before the Queen. Her only suggestion was to add a corsage and the portrait

LEFT **A 1961 stamp depicting the Queen and Prince Andrew**

ABOVE **Pietro Annigoni's romanticised portrait of the Queen**

TOP Arnold Machin
refining the detail of
the image which would
form the portrait for the
new definitive series

was then complete. The bas-relief was photographed countless times in varying lighting conditions to achieve just the right shading effect for the modelling.

Meanwhile, the design for the portrait's frame also occupied Machin. Interestingly, he moved from a fairly decorative border complete with the words 'Postage' and 'Revenue' to the utterly stripped-back design featuring just the portrait and stamp value that we know so well today.

On 5 June 1967, the same week that The Beatles released their magnum opus, the *Sergeant Pepper* album, the first three low-value definitives were issued – the 4d olive-brown sepia, 1s violet and 1s 9d black and orange. The colour of the 4d stamp had been specified by the Queen because of its similarity to the Penny Black, however it was later changed to red for operational reasons. Eventually 14 colours were chosen as the palette for the low-value range. The reaction of the public and collectors to the new stamps was unanimous – they were universally praised for their elegance, simplicity and dignity.

Machin continued to work on the stamp series through the period of decimalisation in the early 1970s and went on to design the commemorative Crown coins for the Royal Silver Wedding of 1972 and the Silver Jubilee of 1977. The Machin image appeared on all coins minted until 1985. In retirement,

Machin moved to Staffordshire where he used his design skills making beautiful gardens with grottoes and cascades. He received an OBE in 1965 and died in 1999 aged 87.

The Machin stamp is now widely recognised as a design classic and an icon of the UK. In 2007 its fortieth birthday was marked by a stamp issue featuring a new ruby colour for the £1 stamp and by two commemorative stamps, one reproducing the original 4d value and the other featuring a portrait of Arnold Machin: the first time a stamp designer has been so honoured. From January 2008 the Machin is Royal Mail's longest-running continuous stamp design, beating the Penny Black/twopence blue.

ARNOLD MACHIN 1911-1999

ABOVE AND BELOW **Stamps celebrating the 40th birthday of the Machin definitive**

LEFT **Work in progress in Machin's studio**

FIRST MACHIN ISSUED 1967

THE FACE ON THE COINS

Ever since the Penny Black established the precedent, the image of the monarch has always faced to his or her right on UK definitive stamps. This is unlike the image on that other vehicle for the iconic portrait of the reigning monarch: the coinage. Following centuries of tradition, successive monarchs face in opposite directions on the Royal Mint's coinage. Days before the first definitive stamps of Queen Elizabeth's reign were issued in December 1952, the new portrait of Her Majesty, facing right, was approved (1). This profile by Mary Gillick was used on all coinage until its replacement by the effigy by Arnold Machin RA, approved in 1964 (2). The portrait featured the Queen in corsage similar to Machin's later design for the definitive stamp, and was used on all the decimal coins introduced from 1968. Raphael Maklouf FRSA created the next effigy, adopted in 1985, and featuring Her Majesty wearing a crown (3). The fourth portrait on British coins was the result of a specialist competition run by the Mint, where from 19 entries a portrait by Ian Rank-Broadley FRBS FSNAD was selected (4). Introduced in 1998, Rank-Broadley expressed the hope that he had struck the right balance between the traditions of the past and the spirit of the present. The Queen is depicted wearing the same tiara as featured on the Machin effigy which had appeared 30 years before.

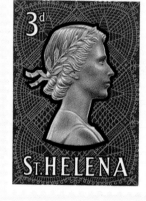

The Royal Mint also produces the Royal Maundy for the monarch to distribute every Maundy Thursday. This ancient ceremony features the distribution of silver Maundy coins to as many elderly men and women as there are years in the sovereign's reign. Although the image of the Queen on the ordinary circulating coinage has appeared in four incarnations, the reverse of the Maundy money bears the original portrait of Her Majesty prepared by Gillick for the very first coins issued in 1953 (left).

ROYAL TELEVISION

The BBC had approached the Queen to televise the Christmas message in 1954, but she declined. It was not until 1958 that the Queen's Christmas broadcast was televised for the first time – live. Holes were drilled through walls at the Palace for TV cables, letting in icy drafts. 'Everyone thought it was nerves but actually I was frozen,' recalled the Queen. Apparently the Queen had an attack of giggles before the transmission, but composed herself for the live broadcast. When complete, thinking the transmission was over, the Queen gave her husband a broad smile. Unknown to her, she was still on air.

In 1966, the process of changing the style of the monarchy was in place. On Christmas Day, an hour-long documentary, *The Royal Palaces of Britain,* was screened – and for the first time the public was allowed a view of the 'inner sanctums' of the royal family. This was a foretaste of what was to come. In June 1969 some 23 million British viewers tuned into *Royal Family*. This landmark programme, which involved 75 days of filming, showed the most intimate portrait yet of the Queen and her family. The programme showed the family as it had never been seen before – off-duty. Memorable scenes include the family enjoying a barbecue by a loch, and celebrating Christmas at Windsor. For many viewers, the most memorable feature of the film was the emergence of members of the family as individuals and personalities. After this milestone, media access to the monarch and her family could only become more insistent.

A week after the *Royal Family* broadcast, viewers were able to enjoy the ceremony of the investiture of the Prince of Wales. Media aware, the Queen decided that there would not be a Christmas broadcast that year, apparently on the grounds that there was a risk of royalty over-exposure. However, there was a public outcry – the Queen's broadcast is, after all, one of the defining features of Christmas Day.

Distinguished TV executive and critic Milton Shulman praised the reception of the film and noted: 'An old image has been replaced by a fresh one. The emphasis on authority and remoteness which was the essence of the previous image has, ever since George VI, been giving way to a friendlier image of homeliness, industry and relaxation.' Yet he warned, 'Every institution that has so far attempted to use TV to popularise or aggrandise itself has been trivialised by it.' A media precedent had been set, but media access to the royal family had to be managed.

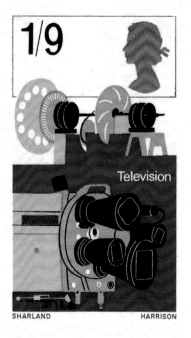

Tywysog Cymru 1969 Prince of Wales

ABOVE AND OPPOSITE **The 1969 David Gentleman stamps celebrating the investiture of the Prince of Wales, including Prince Charles' first appearance on a UK stamp**

Prince Charles, born into the baby-boomer generation, had grown up in the 1960s. He had been sent to his father's old prep school at Cheam and then to Gordonstoun in Scotland, the first Heir Apparent to be educated among other children. A taste of the media exposure to come was underlined by the young Prince Charles' experience in 1963. On a Gordonstoun school expedition to the Isle of Lewis, he and other boys were given permission to visit the local cinema. In the street, the Prince was recognized and a crowd began to gather. The Prince's detective took the boys to a local hotel for privacy while he went to get the cinema tickets, but bystanders began to look through the hotel windows. An uncomfortable 15-year-old Prince Charles moved to an adjacent room to escape their gaze, only to find that he had walked into the hotel bar. To cover his confusion he is reported to have ordered the first drink that came to mind, a cherry brandy, 'Because I'd drunk it before when it was cold out shooting'. Almost inevitably, a journalist entered the bar at that moment with the predictable consequences: newspaper reports of the heir to the throne's under-age attendance at a bar and speculation on discipline at Gordonstoun, as well as the Prince's upbringing.

By the time of his investiture at Caernarfon Castle in 1969, he was a 20-year-old Cambridge undergraduate living in rooms in college like every other student. The Prince of Wales appeared for the first time on a UK stamp to mark the investiture which launched him into public life. The Earl Marshal, the Duke of Norfolk, was in charge of the arrangements. When asked at a press conference what would happen if it rained on the day the Duke made a characteristic observation: 'If it rains we shall all get wet'. But despite the Duke's comment of 'there will be no monkeying about in the name of modernisation', the staging of the investiture was both striking and had a contemporary slant. Lord Snowdon, Constable of Caernarfon Castle, site of the investiture, was asked to design the setting of the site as well as some of the costumes. The mix of antiquity and modernity drew widespread praise.

Yet, the event had been dogged by the threat of disruption from Welsh nationalists. Security was so tight that even Princess Margaret had her handbag checked. But the ceremony passed without major incident as 19 million viewers in Britain and 500 million around the world watched Charles take the oath of allegiance to the Queen (the same oath his father had made in Westminster Abbey following the coronation) as she buckled on his sword and placed the princely coronet on his head. She led him to the castle balcony known as Queen Eleanor's gate and presented him to the Welsh people as 'My most dear son'. The BBC produced a mammoth six-hour television programme using 30 cameras. The student prince was now the Prince of Wales.

A Silver
Decade

1970s

'I have seen from a unique position of advantage, the great phase of the transformation of the Empire into Commonwealth and the transformation  of the Crown from an emblem of domination into a symbol of free and voluntary association. In all history, this has no precedent. In 1947 I pledged my life to the service of our people and I asked for God's help to make good that vow. Although that vow was made in my salad days when I was green in judgement, I do not regret nor retract one word of it. '

GUILDHALL SPEECH
TO CELEBRATE THE
SILVER JUBILEE, JUNE 1977

TIMELINE

1970

Tour of Australia and New Zealand, visiting Fiji and Tonga en route, with Princess Anne, and accompanied by the Prince of Wales for part of the time

Visit to Canada with Prince of Wales and Princess Anne

1971

Visit to Canada with Princess Anne to attend centennial celebrations of the province of British Columbia

State visit to Turkey

Received state visits from Emperor Hirohito of Japan and King Zahir Shah of Afghanistan

1972

Tour to Thailand, Singapore, Malaysia, Brunei, the Maldive Islands, the Seychelles, Mauritius and Kenya

State visits to France and Yugoslavia

Received state visits from Queen Juliana of the Netherlands, Grand Duke Jean of Luxembourg and President Heineman of the Federal Republic of Germany

Silver wedding of the Queen and Prince Philip

1973

Visit to Canada

Visit to Australia to open Sydney Opera House

Marriage of Princess Anne and Captain Mark Phillips

1974

Visit to Cook Islands, tour of New Zealand and attendance of Commonwealth Games

Visits to Norfolk Island, New Hebrides, British Solomon Islands, Papua New Guinea and then tour of Australia where Her Majesty opened Parliament

State visit to Indonesia, returning to Britain via Singapore

1975

Visit to Bermuda, Barbados and Bahamas

State visit to Mexico

Visit to Jamaica during meeting of Commonwealth Heads of Government

State visit to Japan, also visiting Hawaii, Guam and Hong Kong en route

1976

State visits to Finland and Luxembourg

State visit to United States in connection with bicentennial celebrations

Visit to Nova Scotia and New Brunswick before opening and attending Olympic Games in Montreal (Princess Anne competed with British team in equestrian event)

1977

Silver Jubilee tours of Western Samoa, Fiji, Tonga, Papua New Guinea, Australia and New Zealand

Visit to Federal Republic of Germany for Silver Jubilee Review of British Army at Sennelager

Silver Jubilee tours of Canada, Bahamas, Antigua, British Virgin Islands and Barbados

1978

State visit to Federal Republic of Germany, including visits to Bonn, Mainz, Berlin, Bremerhaven and Bremen

Visited Canada and attended Commonwealth Games

1979

Visit to Saudia Arabia, Kuwait, Bahrain, Qatar, United Arab Emirates and Oman

State visits to Denmark, Tanzania, Malawi, Botswana and Zambia

The 1970s was a decade of confrontation. They were unnerving years, marked by an upsurge in terrorism at home and abroad. At the Munich Olympics in 1972 Israeli athletes were tragically murdered by Palestinian terrorists, and hostages were killed during attempts to free them. In the same year the unrest in Northern Ireland escalated, as British troops opened fire on protest marchers on 'Bloody Sunday' in Londonderry. For the royal family the sectarian violence which characterized the decade culminated in personal tragedy when Earl Mountbatten, Prince Philip's uncle and close advisor to the Queen and Prince Charles, was killed by an IRA bomb in 1979. In his diary the Prince of Wales wrote that 'life will never be the same now that he has gone'.

It was a decade of conflict in British industry. The days lost through strikes and go-slows reached an all-time high. Life was made difficult by an oil crisis and rapid inflation and new challenges were presented by the move to decimal coinage and Britain's entry into the European Community. In spite or, perhaps, because of this uncertainty and national belt-tightening the British celebrated the Queen's Silver Jubilee with real enthusiasm. The Queen herself, whose finances were under discussion by Parliament, was averse to great shows of expensive pomp to mark her 25 years on the throne. Instead the event prompted a spontaneous nationwide outpouring of patriotism and street-partying.

The new music to orchestrate a changing Britain was punk. As a noisy, violent reaction to the smooth hair and flared trousers of disco dancers, punks glued their hair into wild spikes and safety pins became high fashion. By the 1970s women's dreams about liberation had become a social and legal fight against the restraints of life, both at work and in the home. In 1979 Mrs Thatcher stormed to the centre of politics, becoming the country's first woman Prime Minister and setting the scene for the revolution that was to continue to roll through the 1980s.

THE SILVER WEDDING

In tune with the changes in how royalty was perceived, the informal dignity of the Royal Silver Wedding stamp image in 1972 demonstrated that royal grandeur and remoteness were giving way to an emphasis on domesticity and accessibility. The Queen and Prince Philip are shown in profile, close up and with no trace of royal decoration. To mark the occasion of their Silver Wedding anniversary there was a thanksgiving service at Westminster Abbey, followed by a lunch at the Guildhall. Once again underlining the new, relaxed tone of the modern monarchy, the Queen began her speech with humour and alluded to a familiar royal

phrase. 'I think everyone will concede that today, of all occasions, I should begin my speech with "My husband and I".' The celebrations continued with a private party masterminded by Prince Charles and Princess Anne.

A photographic treatment was decided for the Silver Wedding stamps; royal and society photographer Norman Parkinson was commissioned. The elegant design by Jeffery Matthews had to take into account that Elizabeth had been a princess at the time of her marriage in 1947; although the image carries an

RIGHT **Jeffery Matthews'
preliminary designs for
the Silver Wedding
stamps and the issued
stamp (below)**

OPPOSITE **The royal family
visit stamp printers
Harrison & Sons to see
the Silver Wedding issue
being printed**

RIGHT **Royal signatures on
the proofed stamps**

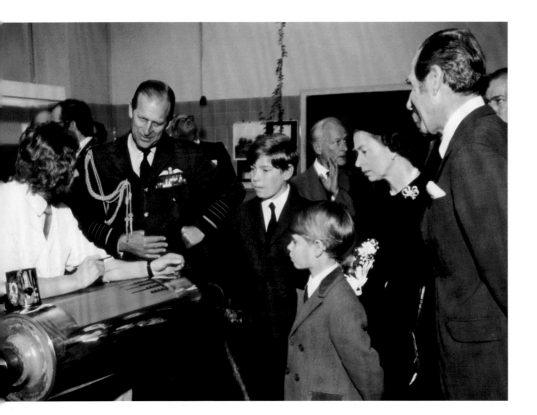

WALKABOUT

The year 1970 marked a new phase in the Queen's life as well as the life of the country. The TV documentary *Royal Family* had added to the expectation that the monarchy would be less remote and that media access would increase. On the political scene, Harold Wilson was defeated in the June election and was succeeded by Edward Heath and the Conservatives, whose priority was for UK entry into the EEC. Objections to the UK being admitted continued so long as its links with the Commonwealth remained. Australia and New Zealand, for example, greatly valued the trade links with Britain and did not seek change, but republicanism in these countries was a growing pressure. A royal tour to Australasia was therefore timely and a new experiment to bring monarchy nearer to the people was tried – the royal walkabout. This consisted of the Queen, at selected locations, walking close to large crowds rather than passing in a motorcade. The first walkabout was in Wellington, New Zealand, and the Queen stopped and chatted many times, close enough to the public to receive gifts and flowers. The *Daily Mail* coined the term 'walkabout' from the wanderings of indigenous Australian Aborigines – although the term actually refers to an activity to get away from civilization. The tour was a huge success, and the people of Australasia experienced a royal family that was warm and human. Walkabouts were used to memorable extent in the following year of Her Majesty and Prince Philip's Silver Wedding.

unmistakeable sense of the monarchy, the theme is handled lightly. Surprisingly, this was also the first depiction of the Duke of Edinburgh on a British stamp. Almost six months before the issue date, the Queen, Prince Philip and their sons Princes Andrew and Edward made their first visit to a stamp printer and attended the printing of the stamps at Harrison & Sons (now De La Rue) in High Wycombe.

Their anniversary year was also key in the increasing media interest in the family and in November the first paparazzi to make a serious living from photographing the British royals published a picture book to coincide with the Silver Wedding. It was called *To Tread on Royal Toes*. Ray Belissario was known as the 'Peeping Tom the Royals Dread' and he was very successful at selling pictures, not least one of Princess Margaret in a swimsuit which he sold for an extraordinary £25,000.

JEFFERY MATTHEWS: DESIGNER

'It's a job that works both the head and the heart,' says Jeffery Matthews in describing the task of designing stamps. In more than four decades of working with Royal Mail he has designed more than 40 Special Stamps and has been involved in the design of the classic Machin definitive. He is renowned for his work on royal and heraldic stamps. Indeed it was the rich colour, and the order and complexity of heraldic imagery that initially drew him to study design.

The first Matthews-designed stamps were issued by Royal Mail in 1965 to mark the 20th anniversary of the United Nations as well as International Co-operation Year. In 1972 his first royal commemorative stamp marked the Queen and Prince Philip's Silver Wedding and has been followed by many others with royal themes – including issues for the Queen's 60th birthday and the wedding of Prince Charles and Lady Diana Spencer. Heraldry has been a continuing theme too. His glorious 1984

issue celebrated the 500th anniversary of the College of Arms – for which he created Royal Mail's first square stamps – and the lavishly

detailed 1998 issue celebrated the Order of the Garter's 650th anniversary, and the 45th anniversary of the coronation. Matthews has also undertaken considerable work in refreshing and updating the Machin definitive and producing post-decimalisation stamps for Northern Ireland, Scotland and Wales, as well as the Isle of Man, each featuring an appropriate emblem juxtaposed with the Machin bas-relief portrait.

Without doubt one of his most popular designs was for the 150th anniversary of the Penny Black in 1990. 'I was a channel for the finest stamp designs of all times,' he says of the work which combined Queen Victoria's head from the original Penny Black with the Machin bas-relief of our present Queen. As ever the work was painstakingly executed, paying heed to balance and structure. 'I am always searching for perfection and seldom satisfied,' says Matthews.

BUILDING MODERN BRITAIN

During the 1970s there were no fewer than six sets of stamps devoted to British architecture and architects. Some of these celebrated the traditional buildings of Britain: castles and palaces, village churches and country houses. But the stamp issues also reflected the huge amount of new building that was taking place at the time. British city centres were being modernised and restructured. Planners – taking account of the rapid growth in car ownership – presided over endless ring-road, flyover and bypass schemes. Architects – especially those with a fondness for the 'brutalist' concrete that was de rigueur at the time – were busy constructing tower blocks for living and working.

Later, the uncompromising style of many of these buildings came in for criticism, but in 1971 the stamps showing Modern University Buildings were clearly issued in a spirit of optimism. Typical of the modernist architectural style of the age, these buildings also illustrated the rapid expansion of higher education. Since the violent protests in Paris in 1968, students had been much in the news and were a target for the popular press. When the Queen visited Stirling University in 1972 much was made of the fact that she was allegedly jostled by protesting students, although

the news pictures of the day merely show a smiling Queen passing some young people lolling around drinking what looks like alcohol straight from the bottle.

In 1975 the new National Theatre featured as part of the stamp set marking European Architectural Heritage Year. The Queen officially opened Denys Lasdun's long-awaited building on the South Bank a year later, in October 1976 – a full 25 years after Queen Elizabeth, the Queen Mother had laid the foundation stone. The opening production was *Hamlet*, with Albert Finney playing the title role. But not everyone was happy with the finished theatre. Associate director Jonathan Miller resigned, saying the building 'looked like a mixture of Gatwick airport and Brent Cross shopping centre'. The Prince of Wales – a traditionalist who was to become an outspoken critic of modern architecture – has likened the building to a nuclear power station.

THE QUEEN'S PASSION FOR HORSES

The Queen has always been a keen horsewoman. On her fourth birthday she was given her first pony – a Shetland called Peggy – by her doting grandfather, King George V, and the seal was set. Even Madame Tussaud's, wanting to display a wax figure of the young Princess in the 1930s, chose to represent her astride that pony. Horses – whether for the ceremony of state, for breeding and racing or for relaxation and pleasure – have been a vital component of the Queen's life and reign. A love of horses is something the Queen shares with huge numbers of her subjects and this was reflected in the stamp issue of 1978 depicting four of the best-loved British horses – the Shire, the Shetland pony, the Welsh pony and the Thoroughbred.

Horse breeding and the turf, 'the sport of kings', have been a royal passion down the centuries. But Queen Elizabeth has gone further than many of her predecessors. Through her professional expertise and deep knowledge of bloodstock and training she has become a major player in British horse racing, as well as in the breeding of polo ponies, some of which have been ridden in competition by the Prince of Wales. During 1977, the Silver Jubilee year, the Queen was named Top British Breeder of horses. But as early as 1942 the Princess Elizabeth had exhibited what the royal trainer Fred Darling described as 'a natural eye for a horse'. During the 1950s her horses won the George VI and Queen Elizabeth stakes and she became one of the turf's leading winner-owners. Indeed, a few days after her coronation the Queen's horse Aureole came second in the Derby. Her enthusiasm for this race was later shown very eloquently in the TV documentary of 1992, *Elizabeth R*, on the occasion of her 65th birthday. The sequence filmed at Epsom is among the most animated, with the Queen darting forward to watch the race and then winning £16 in the

TOP **The 1978 'Horses' issue**

ABOVE **The royal family's evident love of horses shown on a Samoan stamp**

OPPOSITE **The Queen urges on her horse at Epsom, 1992**

OPPOSITE (INSET) **Saluting at Trooping the colour**

ISLE OF MAN

E II R

£2

C. Corlett   1990   Questa

Saddling Mahmoud for The Derby 1936 **9P**

Photography by Jean Luc Benard formed the 'All the Queen's Horses' stamps, 1997. Clockwise from top left: St Patrick, Thompson, River Star, Janus

Royal Box sweepstake. The Queen can only have been delighted, therefore, when in 1979 the 200th running of The Derby was celebrated in a set of four stamps featuring paintings of famous race meetings, and designed by Stuart Rose, former design adviser to The Post Office (left).

Horses for official and ceremonial duties also occupy the Queen. Founded at Hampton Court in the 16th century, the Royal Stud is the world's oldest racehorse breeding centre and has considerably influenced the evolution of the thoroughbred. In answer to the problem of finding suitable drum horses for the Household Cavalry, the Queen founded a project at the Royal Stud to breed horses for this unique duty. Janus, a contemporary drum horse, was photographed for the 1997 stamps 'All the Queen's Horses', along with Thompson, another Household Cavalry horse. The Monarch has a unique relationship with the Household Cavalry. She is Colonel-in-Chief and the Cavalry escort her on state occasions. Just south of Buckingham Palace, up to 34 horses are stabled at the Royal Mews which is responsible for the conveyance of the royal family by road. Two horses from these stables were also photographed for the 'All the Queens Horses' set – River Star, a 20-year-old elder statesman of a horse who was reserved for Prince Philip to ride at Trooping the Colour, and St Patrick, an imposing Irish Grey wearing the Number Three State Harness. Special occasions would see St Patrick, coupled with three other horses to the Irish State Coach, taking the Queen and Prince Philip to the State Opening of Parliament. In keeping with tradition, St Patrick was named by the Queen.

PRINCESS ANNE

In many ways the 1970s was Princess Anne's decade. The British public followed stories of her travels and sporting triumphs, her marriage and then motherhood. The early years of the decade saw the princess joining her parents on royal tours to Canada, Turkey and the Far East, before beginning to travel in her own right. In 1973 she became the first member of the royal family to visit the Soviet Union.

Meanwhile, Anne was fast becoming a world-class rider. In 1971, the 21-year-old princess was voted Sportswoman of the Year by the British Sportswriters Association; and, having won the European Three-Day Event championship at Burghley, she was also elected BBC's Sports Personality of the Year. In 1976, she was part of the British equestrian team at the Montreal Olympic Games, which was officially opened by the Queen.

It was through competitive riding that Princess Anne met Mark Philips, who was a lieutenant in the Queen's Dragoons and an Olympic rider. They married on 14 November 1973 (Prince Charles's 25th birthday) and the wedding was marked with two Special Stamps, the first set to be issued in celebration of a royal marriage.

The couple had announced their engagement at the Badminton Horse trials in May. Lord Lichfield, the photographer cousin of the Queen, took the photograph for the stamps that summer. Ironically, it was Lichfield's great-great-grandfather who, as Postmaster General in 1830s, had unsuccessfully opposed Rowland Hill's idea for a pre-paid postage label or 'stamp'.

In 1987 she received the title Princess Royal from the Queen, and today has a high-profile role as President of the Save the Children Fund. Undertaking more than 600 royal engagements a year, she is respected as a hard-working member of the royal family and has been closely involved in the establishment of charities such as The Princess Royal Trust for Carers, and Riders for Health. In 2000 the Queen awarded her daughter the Order of the Thistle in recognition of her work for charities. The Princess is also a member of the International Olympic Committee and took part in London's successful bid to host the 2012 Olympic Games, which Royal Mail celebrated with stamps.

SILVER YEARS

After a succession of difficult years through the first half of the 1970s, it seemed that the nation was ready to forget its troubles and slip into party mood. The 1977 Silver Jubilee marking 25 years since the Queen's accession was the ideal opportunity to celebrate in style. The accession had been in February 1952, but most revelry for the Silver Jubilee took place during the summer. In the first few

ABOVE **The Queen toured the UK as well as the Commonwealth in 1977**

OPPOSITE **Silver Jubilee fever**

OPPOSITE (INSET) **The rose 'Silver Jubilee' appeared on a 1991 stamp**

months of the year the Queen took part in royal tours to Australia and the Pacific, and later to Canada and the Caribbean. In between there was a tour of the United Kingdom which included Northern Ireland, despite the terrorist threat. The date of 7 June was chosen as the official holiday and all around Britain there were carnivals, street parties, parades and pageants. A million people flanked The Mall to watch the State Coach take the Queen and Prince Philip from Buckingham Palace to St Paul's Cathedral. An appearance on the balcony of Buckingham Palace was greeted by a crowd numbering 500,000 – more than appeared on the historic VE night in 1945. Even a hybrid tea-rose was named in honour of the year and won coveted trophies from the Royal National Rose Society. The 'Silver Jubilee' rose was later to grace a UK stamp.

The Queen's image appeared everywhere, including plastic bags, T-shirts, hologram pendants and commemorative mugs and plates (a visual riposte, perhaps, to the anarchic image of Her Majesty made famous by the punk rock band The Sex Pistols). As an added bonus, Virginia Wade won Wimbledon that year and was presented with the trophy by the Queen, and later Her Majesty became a grandmother when Princess Anne's son Peter Phillips was born. A cropped version of the Lord Snowdon portrait of the proud grandmother was used in the 2002 Golden Jubilee stamps issue.

Rosa Silver Jubilee

22

DESIGNING SPECIAL EDITIONS

In 1839 Sir Rowland Hill set up a competition to design the world's first adhesive postage stamp. It generated around 2600 entries, none of which were felt suitable. Finally, he entrusted the task to three members of the Royal Academy, who came up with the Penny Black. Thankfully, Royal Mail went on to establish a more streamlined approach to its stamp design. When a Special Stamp theme is decided upon, detailed research into the subject area begins and possible angles and treatments emerge. Design staff are familiar with the work of a huge range of artists, illustrators, photographers and graphic designers and can match their skills with thestyle and treatment desired. Up to three different designers are separately briefed and commissioned, each asked to pursue a different approach to the subject. After consultation and preliminary work, 'presentation visuals' are delivered to take to the Royal Mail Stamp Advisory Committee (SAC). This body was established in its present form in 1968 and meets around nine times a year to review the stamp designs underway. British stamps have a world-wide reputation for originality and the SAC aims to keep it that way. It is a body of up to a dozen individuals from the worlds of design, art, philately and the media, and they provide a testing ground for stamp ideas and decide on which of the three routes devised for an issue should go forward to finalization and production. The Queen, however, has to approve the final proofs before a stamp is issued.

Compared with the high-profile excitement of the Silver Jubilee, the 1978 anniversary of the coronation passed off quietly. In terms of stamp design the Silver Jubilee was marked by a single, simple design by Richard Guyatt. This featured a central portrait of the Queen flanked by large letters 'E' and 'R' – a set of five were issued in different colours for the different values. The coronation anniversary designs by Jeffery Matthews were a delicate and understated quartet featuring motifs of the coronation including the State Coach and the Orb printed in gold against a richly coloured backdrop.

ENTRY INTO EUROPE

Edward Heath was the Prime Minister who oversaw Britain's entry into the Common Market. The Treaty of Accession became effective on 1 January 1973 and there was a Special Stamp issue to mark the occasion. That stamp image suggested that Britain was a natural part of the jigsaw of European nations. In fact there was – and remains – a fierce debate across the political parties about just how snugly the country should fit into the European Community. On the day he signed the papers Edward Heath was drenched in black ink by a woman protestor worried about what she saw as Britain's relinquishment of power to Brussels.

In the 1960s Charles de Gaulle had vetoed British membership of the EC. The Queen and the royal family had been part of the effort to win him round during an impressive state visit in 1960. All the stops were pulled out for the French President – open-top carriage rides with the Queen, a state banquet and a gala evening at Covent Garden for which Cecil Beaton decked the opera house with 25,000 pink carnations (a gesture that came to be known as the Fantasy of Flowers). De Gaulle went away with a very favourable view of royal hospitality, but with his mind unchanged on Britain's entry into Europe. When Britain was allowed into the EC it was on disadvantageous terms – high budget contributions, a poor deal for British fishermen and a costly agricultural policy.

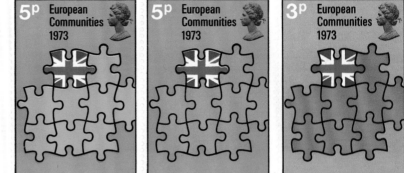

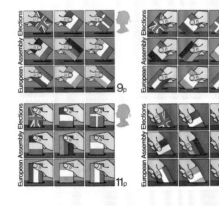

Nevertheless the cultural effects of Britain's closer relationship with the Continent were more auspicious. Britain was becoming less insular. The number of people taking package holidays went up by half – to 8.5 million in the first three years of the 1970s. The British developed a taste for pizza, paella, pasta and plonk. Later, under Harold Wilson in 1975, the first referendum in British history was held on Britain's continued membership of the EC. The electorate voted 'yes' overwhelmingly. By 1979 – when the first direct elections to European Assembly were marked with a brightly graphic set of stamps based on a grid of the flags of the nine member states – the anti-marketeers looked as though they had been defeated, although they would rise to fight another day.

More than a decade later, with the birth of the European Union in 1992, Royal Mail celebrated in style with a vibrant David Hockney-designed stamp.

Weddings
and Renewal

1980s

'There is no point regretting the passage of time. Growing older is one of the facts of life, and has its own compensations. Experience should help us to take a more balanced view of events and to be more understanding about the foibles of human nature.'

THE QUEEN'S CHRISTMAS
MESSAGE, DECEMBER 1987

45

TIMELINE

1980
State visits to Switzerland, Australia, Italy,
the Vatican, Tunisia, Algeria and Morocco
Visits the European Commission in Belgium
and the North Atlantic Treaty Organisation
Visits the Federal Republic of Germany to inspect
the 1st Battalion of the Royal Welch Fusiliers

1981
State visits to Norway, Australia and New
Zealand and Sri Lanka
Wedding of Prince and Princess of Wales (29 July)

1982
Visits Canada for Patriation Ceremony in Ottawa
and visited Australia (attending
Commonwealth Games at Brisbane), Papua
New Guinea, Solomon Islands, Nauru, Kiribati,
Tuvalu and Fiji
Birth of Prince William (21 June)

1983
Visits Jamaica, Cayman Islands, Mexico, the
United States and Canada
State visits to Sweden, Kenya, Bangladesh
and India

1984
State visit to Jordan and Canada
Visits France to attend ceremonies in Normandy
to mark 40th anniversary of the Allied
Landings (D Day)
Birth of Prince Harry (15 September)

1985
State visit to Portugal
Visits to Belize, Bahamas, St Christopher and
Nevis, Antigua, Dominica, Saint Lucia and Saint
Vincent and the Grenadines, Barbados,
Grenada and Trinidad and Tobago

1986
Visits to Nepal, New Zealand and Australia
State visit to the People's Republic of China
and visited Hong Kong
Marriage of Prince Andrew, Duke of York, to
Sarah Ferguson

1987
Visits Federal Republic of Germany and Canada
(British Columbia at time of the
Commonwealth Heads of Government
meeting, Saskatchewan and Quebec)

1988
Visits Australia in connection with country's
Bicentenary celebrations
Visits the Netherlands and Spain

1989
Visits Barbados in connection with the 350th
anniversary of the Barbados Parliament
Receives state visits from President Babangida
of Nigeria and the President of the United
Arab Emirates
Separation announced of Princess Royal and
Captain Mark Phillips
Visits to Bahrain, Singapore and attended
Commonwealth Heads of Government
conference in Malaysia

The 1980s will doubtless be remembered as the Thatcher years. Mrs Thatcher, the Conservative Prime Minister, dominated the political life of the country. At home there was rioting in British cities in the early 1980s, and unrest in mining communities during the protracted strike.

The 1982 Argentine invasion of the Falkland Islands in the South Atlantic was a breach of the sovereignty of British territory. It prompted a war in which the Queen's son, Prince Andrew, served as a naval officer. As the Task Force approached its destination in the South Atlantic, the danger was real and, alongside countless other British families, the royal family waited anxiously for success and the safe return of their son.

Exposure to danger had become something of a hallmark of public life. The Queen's vulnerability was highlighted when blank shots were fired at her during the 1981 Trooping the Colour ceremony. The intrusion of Michael Fagan into her bedroom at Buckingham Palace the following year was a further shocking breach of royal security. The 1980s saw a continuation of IRA atrocities – the Queen's Household Cavalry was attacked, with soldiers killed and injured as they rode to the Changing of the Guard in 1982. In 1984 the bombing of the Grand Hotel Brighton at the time of the Conservative Party Conference came perilously close to wiping out the entire government.

Yet the 1980s were also, memorably, years of celebration with two royal weddings and the arrival of Princess Diana as the most glamorous star in the royal firmament. In the newly de-regulated City of London trading was fast and money flowed nearly as quickly as the champagne which was drunk in unprecedented amounts. But it wasn't to last. In October 1987 the stock market crashed and many fortunes were lost. Ordinary Britons found themselves owning property that was now worth considerably less than they paid for it. The bubble that was the 1980s had burst.

ROYAL WEDDINGS

On 29 July 1981 the wedding of Prince Charles and Lady Diana Spencer was the wedding to end them all. Theirs was described as a fairytale relationship, with the heir to the throne choosing a young and beautiful wife, who at 19 was 13 years his junior.

Lady Diana, a nursery school teacher at the time of her engagement, was the youngest daughter of the seventh Earl Spencer. The Queen had known Diana since her birth, as Earl Spencer had long been part of the royal household as one of her father's equerries. Diana, too, was no stranger to the royal household – as a child she had been a friend of Prince Andrew who was one year her senior, and there had been speculation that Diana and Andrew might become a couple. However, during the summer of 1979 at Balmoral it was clear that Diana, staying with her sister – whose husband was one of the Queen's assistant private secretaries – had caught the attention of Prince Charles. She appeared at Balmoral the following year, too, and on 6 February 1981 Prince Charles, aged 32, proposed. The country, and then the rest of the world, began its love affair with Diana.

14ᴾ

29 July 1981

Lord Snowdon's portrait of the Prince and Princess of Wales graced the Royal Wedding issue

The wedding was an extraordinary and extravagant event. It was marked by two simple portrait stamps of the couple in relaxed mode looking directly at the camera, designed by Jeffery Matthews. The official engagement photographs had proved to be unsuitable for the stamps, so new photographs were commissioned from Lord Snowdon.

Meanwhile, wedding preparations were lavish, a fairytale lace dress was commissioned from Elizabeth and David Emanuel and a huge TV spectacular

Royal Wedding 29 July 1981

1981   COURVOISIER

MAURITIUS   R5

was planned. The dress itself became a much copied garment for weddings for months afterwards. Some 600,000 people lined the route to St Paul's Cathedral and around the world more than a billion people watched the event on their television screens. The crowning moment was the couple's kiss on the balcony of Buckingham Palace – the world swooned at the romance. As the Archbishop of Canterbury said in his address during the ceremony, the day was the stuff of which fairytales were made.

Five years later came the marriage of Prince Andrew and Sarah Ferguson. Prince Andrew had won the nation's admiration in the early 1980s for his courage as an active member of the Task Force during the Falklands War. He became a helicopter pilot with 820 Sea King Squadron aboard HMS *Invincible* and accepted the dangers of acting as decoy for the devastating Exocet missiles as part of his job. On his return to Britain he remained in the newspaper headlines with a succession of romances. Finally, his name was linked with

23 JULY 1986

Jeffery Matthews' stamp design for Prince Andrew and Sarah Ferguson's wedding featured a Gene Nocon portrait

Sarah Ferguson and in 'the worst kept secret of the year' Prince Andrew and Sarah Ferguson faced the TV cameras together for the first time to talk publicly about their romance in March 1986.

This second royal marriage of the 1980s was a rather different affair from the first – Andrew was not heir to the throne. The commemorative stamps were again designed by Jeffery Matthews, this time using a photograph by Gene Nocon. The issue was even more informal than the Charles and Diana imagery, with Prince Andrew dressed casually in open-necked shirt and jumper and Sarah – already nicknamed 'Fergie' – in regular day clothes. On the morning of the wedding the Prince was created Duke of York and it was as Duke and Duchess that the couple left Westminster Abbey. Once again it was a theatrical occasion and once again there was a kiss on the balcony of Buckingham Palace, although the event failed to quite match the fervour of Charles and Diana's wedding.

Through the 1980s, the younger generation of royals established themselves, and the media's appetite for stories and photos increased. The Prince and Princess of Wales' first child, Prince William, was born in June 1982 and a precedent was set when the young prince accompanied his parents on an Australasian tour in 1983. The Prince and Princess of Wales drew vast, enthusiastic crowds. The international appeal of royalty seemed greater than ever in the 1980s and the younger generation even began to set standards of fashion. Diana herself extended royal patronage to the British fashion industry and her distinctive layered blonde hair was readily copied.

The Prince and Princess of Wales with baby Prince William on a 1982 Mauritius stamp – his first appearance on a stamp

R2·50 Mauritius

Birth of HRH Prince William of Wales

ALL CHANGE

It is hard to imagine a set of postage stamps that could have been more pertinent at the beginning of the 1980s than the two Information Technology stamps issued in 1982. The stamps celebrated the development of communications and new digital technology – their unusual landscape-format design showed illustrations of computers, barcodes, information technology and satellite communications – all of which presaged a profound change in our lives and a boom in the service and financial sectors during Mrs Thatcher's administration. This was the decade of IT and the enterprise culture.

In the 1980s, more than ever before, the Queen was asked to make royal trips abroad with an emphasis less on promoting good relations with the Commonwealth countries and beyond, and more on fostering trade relations. Royal tours reached unprecedented levels in this era. As Prince Philip commented in an interview in 1983: 'The late King only went abroad twice – to Canada and South Africa. Look what happens to us – we're abroad somewhere in the Commonwealth every year, and we go to other countries as well. The ease of travel means you are asked to do more things.'

ABOVE **The new world of technology appears in the 1982 Information Technology stamp issue**

OPPOSITE **Industrial archaeology miniature sheet designed by Ronald Maddox**

These were the years during which Britain, along with many other Western countries, was making the painful transition into the post-industrial world and seeing the inexorable decline of heavy industries such as steel, shipbuilding and coal. It was a tremendous sadness that the economic shift left certain parts of the country, most notably the North, disadvantaged and behind in the race to enter the new economic world. The gap between North and South, rich and poor widened.

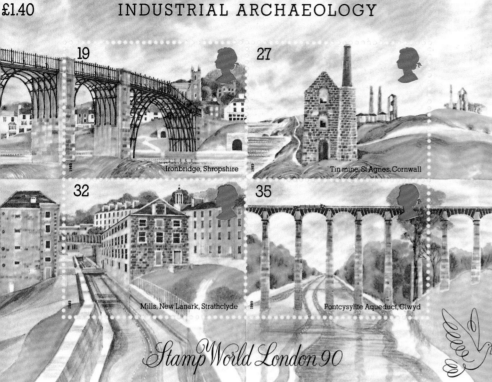

£1.40

INDUSTRIAL ARCHAEOLOGY

19 · Ironbridge, Shropshire

27 · Tin mine, St Agnes, Cornwall

32 · Mills, New Lanark, Strathclyde

35 · Pontcysyllte Aqueduct, Clwyd

Stamp World London 90

The most unattractive representative of the South's new found wealth was the comic character invented by Harry Enfield – 'Loadsamoney'. Here was the archetypal 'Essex man' who had made a fortune and insisted on waving his wad around. 'Loadsamoney' brought home the point that, in some quarters in the 1980s, greed had become acceptable.

Attitudes to our industrial past changed very quickly. The Big Pit in Wales opened as a tourist attraction and was manned by the very miners who had recently worked there digging coal. Canals, mills, industrial buildings and factories found new uses as the 'dark satanic' corners of British cities were cleaned up. By 1989, when the Industrial Archaeology stamp set was issued, we needed little reminder that many of the industries such as tin, cotton and iron – on which Britain once depended – were now largely history.

DUKE OF EDINBURGH AWARDS

One of the highest profile royal charities is the Duke of Edinburgh's Award. It was founded in 1956 with the mission 'to provide for young people an enjoyable, challenging and rewarding programme of personal

development, which is of the highest quality and the widest reach'. More than two million people in over 50 countries have taken part since its inception. Perhaps more than anything else, this challenging programme demonstrates the Duke's keen interest in and support for the personal development of young people. He has been the scheme's patron and Chairman of Trustees since its beginning, and devotes much time presenting Gold awards and meeting both participants and helpers in the UK and overseas.

The scheme – for young people aged between 15 and 25 – is in operation around the world. It attracts tens of thousands of young participants who every year undertake a vast range of activities developing team-working abilities, learning new skills, helping in the community and taking part in tough physical challenges. In 1981 the charity celebrated its 25th anniversary. The quartet of stamps which marked the occasion adopted an illustrative approach, showing the scheme's main areas of activity – namely expeditions, skills, service and recreation.

HAPPY BIRTHDAYS

Along with the big set-piece weddings, the 1980s also saw celebrations for two important royal birthdays – the Queen's 60th and the Queen Mother's 80th.

The Queen Mother's birthday was the first to be celebrated, in August 1980. The commemorative stamp features a regal photographic portrait by Norman Parkinson of Her Majesty sporting a hat of rich turquoise plumage. The photograph by Norman Parkinson captures the features for which the Queen Mum is renowned – her smile, her hats and her pearls. The border of the stamp bears an inscription which was hand-drawn by veteran designer Jeffery Matthews. Amazingly, this was the Queen Mother's first appearance on a British stamp since her Silver Wedding of 1948 which featured a Dorothy Wilding image. It was also the first British stamp to celebrate a royal birthday.

Jeffery Mathews' 60th birthday tribute to the Queen

In April 1986 the Queen's 60th birthday was commemorated with a pair of stamps also designed by Matthews. Each stamp is divided into three segments, one for each decade of her life. The pair provides a linear portrayal of her life, from blonde, curly haired two-year-old child to a Queen who had served her country as its sovereign for more than 30 years. A potential problem in the design was that the portrait on the right of each stamp had to be 'postally' recognisable – these stamps did not require the usual small-scale silhouette of the Queen's head, but did have to meet Royal Mail requirements. In the event the third portrait on the first stamp was that known as the Wilding portrait and the second stamp featured a recent portrait by Lord Snowdon.

Other images included a Cecil Beaton portrait of the 16-year-old Princess during the War, as well as portraits from 1968 and 1973, the latter showing the Queen with camera at the ready at the Badminton Horse Trials. Such was the instant success of the designs that when they were presented to the Stamp Advisory Committee, the whole room burst into spontaneous applause.

ABOVE **Norman Parkinson's photograph of the Queen Mother in the UK birthday stamp**

LEFT **Commonwealth nations' tributes to the royal family, including the Swaziland stamp featuring Norman Parkinson's portrait of the Queen Mother and her daughters**

URBAN RENEWAL

In the same summer as Charles and Diana's wedding – and in stark contrast to it – riots exploded on the streets of Liverpool, London and Bristol. In poorer areas unrest was

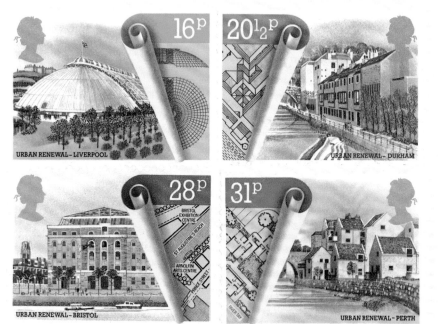

ignited by a combination of economic recession, a sudden rise in unemployment, racial prejudice, poor policing, crime and the decline in standards of housing and public services. In the wake of the riots Lord Scarman produced a report, which, although defending the measures taken by the police to contain the riots, was critical of police training and the force's tendency towards racial discrimination. He called on the government to 'eliminate the basic flaws in our society' and particularly to regenerate the disadvantaged inner cities.

In response to this Michael Heseltine, the Environment Secretary, was entrusted with the task of regenerating the poorer areas of Liverpool. The 'Minister for Merseyside', as he was known, aimed to do this through a radical partnership of government and private enterprise. Local enterprise agencies and urban development corporations became commonplace throughout the country. The Urban Renewal stamps issued in 1984 which brought together new projects in Liverpool, Durham, Bristol and Perth reflected the efforts of these organisations to improve housing and retailing as well as public buildings and amenities and featured illustrations by Ronald Maddox (left).

By end of 1980s, Glasgow – another city that was no stranger to poverty and strife – was ready for what was to become one of the most successful makeovers in British urban history. The beginning of that success, when Glasgow was named as European City of Culture in 1990, was duly celebrated with illustrations by Paul Hogarth RA in a stamp issue that paid tribute to two of Glasgow's most handsome buildings, as well as Royal Mail's British Philatelic Bureau in Edinburgh and Alexandra Palace in north London – the venue for the international stamp exhibition that year.

THE PHOTOGRAPHER PRINCE

In the late 1980s it was decided that a new set of high-value definitive stamps was needed. The idea was to add a sense of importance to those stamps with high face values – from £1 to £5 – and therefore differentiate them from the low-value definitives. For the second time in the Queen's reign, the theme of castles was chosen as the subject matter. In fact, the stamps would feature the very same quartet of castles portrayed in the 1955 issue – Caernarfon, Carrickfergus, Edinburgh and Windsor. However the visual treatment of these handsome subjects was to be entirely different.

The 1955 set had been painted by Lynton Lamb; now it was the turn of enthusiastic amateur photographer the Duke of York. The Duke adopted a bold style of photography using

close-up images of parts of the castles. There was no attempt to show the entire building, instead portions of the structures are highlighted. The photographs were used as the basis of the design, which was engraved. The images were used to occupy most of the stamp frame leaving just enough space for the Queen's silhouette, the value and the name of the castle. The stamps were issued in 1988.

Four years after their first issue, the stamps were updated. With modern copying equipment it had become easier for forgers to duplicate bank notes and stamps, so Royal Mail took the opportunity to build in a number of security features to foil their attempts at counterfeiting. The finished stamps – issued in 1992 – include the use of optically variable ink for the silhouette of the Queen (it varied from gold to green when viewed from different angles).

£1

CARRICKFERGUS CASTLE

£1⁵⁰

CAERNARFON CASTLE

£2

EDINBURGH CASTLE

£5

WINDSOR CASTLE

Decade
'Horribilis'

1990s

'Since I came to the throne in 1952, ten Prime Ministers have served the British people and have come to see me each week at Buckingham Palace. The first, Winston Churchill, had charged with the cavalry at Omdurman. You, Prime Minister, were born in the year of my coronation.'

65

QUEEN'S SPEECH MARKING HER
GOLDEN WEDDING ANNIVERSARY,
NOVEMBER 1997

TIMELINE

1990

Visit to New Zealand to attend
Commonwealth Games
Attended concert at Royal Albert Hall to
mark 50th anniversary of the Battle of Britain
Received President of Colombia and his wife
at Windsor Castle
Visit to Canada

1991

State visit to Namibia and Zimbabwe; opened
the Commonwealth heads of government
meeting in Harare
Visit to USA

1992

Television documentary *Elizabeth R*
Visits to Australia, Malta, France, Canada
and Germany
Duke and Duchess of York separate
The Queen addressed the European Parliament
in Strasbourg for the first time
Receives the Sultan of Brunei and President
Yeltsin of Russia
The Princess Royal marries Commander
Timothy Laurence

1993

State visits to Hungary and Cyprus
The Queen and Duke of Edinburgh attended
events in Liverpool to mark the 50th
anniversary of the Battle of the Atlantic
President de Klerk received in audience
at Buckingham Palace
Private visit to Waterloo Battlefield, Belgium
Visit to Royal Engineers in Germany

1994

Tour of eight nations in the West Indies and
Central America
Queen attends D Day commemoration banquet
for heads of state and service of thanksgiving
at Portsmouth Guildhall; service at the Bayeux
war cemetery; a memorial service at Omaha
beach, Normandy
Visit to Russia, the first by a reigning
British monarch
Official tour to Canada

1995

State visit to South Africa
VE Day celebrations in UK
VJ Day commemorations
Visit to New Zealand

1996

Visits to Poland, Czech Republic and Thailand

1997

Visits to Canada
President Mandela of South Africa received
The Queen and the Duke of Edinburgh held a
garden party at Buckingham Palace to mark
their 50th wedding anniversary
Death of Diana, Princess of Wales, in Paris
(31 August)
State visit to Pakistan

1998

Receives the Emperor and Empress of Japan
State visits to Brunei Darussalam, France,
Belgium and Malaysia. The Queen closed the
Commonwealth Games in Kuala Lumpur
President Havel of the Czech Republic received

1999

Prince Edward announced his engagement
to Sophie Rhys-Jones; married on 21 June
State visit to Republic of Korea
The National Assembly for Wales formally
inaugurated by the Queen in Cardiff
The Scottish Parliament opened by the Queen
The Queen awarded a Royal Charter to the
Prince's Trust
State visit to Ghana and visits to South Africa,
Mozambique

After the excesses and conspicuous consumption of the 1980s, the new decade was greeted with hope. The 'caring 1990s' had been ushered in by the fall of the Berlin Wall and Soviet-based communism, yet the invasion of Kuwait by Iraq and the ensuing Gulf War was the first test of a 'new world order'.

In Britain, the early 1990s also saw the worst economic recession since the 1930s and the resignation of Mrs Thatcher. John Major was chosen as her successor – and the ninth Prime Minister of the Queen's reign.

In 1992 the Queen visited Australia for the 150th anniversary of the founding of Sydney. Republicanism had gathered pace in Australia. The relatively muted reception for this royal tour was in sharp contrast to the post-coronation tour almost 40 years earlier, when 75 per cent of Australians turned out to see the Queen. Much more successful was her 1995 trip to South Africa, where the Queen was warmly welcomed by the country's new President, Nelson Mandela.

But the royal decade was dominated by domestic crises, royal marriages – and by the media obsession with Princess Diana in particular. The 40th anniversary year of the accession, in 1992, proved to be a grim year for the Queen. In March, the Duke and Duchess of York separated and in April the divorce of Princess Anne and Mark Phillips was announced. In November there was a terrible fire at Windsor Castle, which blazed through a sequence of state apartments. The year concluded with the December announcement of the separation of the Prince and Princess of Wales.

In her anniversary speech at London's Guildhall, the Queen said with masterful understatement that '1992 is not a year on which I shall look back with undiluted pleasure. It has turned out to be an annus horribilis.' She could hardly have predicted how much more drama would unfold during the remainder of the decade and how the intense media focus on the Princess of Wales would culminate in the tragedy of her death and the extraordinary show of public emotion.

GALLANTRY AND HONOURS

Britain is renowned around the world for its traditions of pageantry, ceremony and spectacle. Few countries can rival its panoply of public events, which are executed with grandeur and precision. Even detractors have to acknowledge that these displays remain an almost inextricable part of the national identity and the international image of Britain.

One aspect of this heritage is the royal ceremonies held throughout the year for bestowing honours – either to reward loyal service, in recognition of an act of extraordinary courage and valour, or to celebrate a remarkable success. An award from the Queen is still considered by most people to be not just highly treasured, but the greatest honour in the land.

Royal Mail has issued many stamps to celebrate honours and gallantry, as well as many exploring the iconography of heraldry. The intricate, exquisitely designed and richly coloured emblems make ideal subjects for the 'Special Issues'. April 1990 saw the issue of a quartet of stamp designs to mark the 25th Anniversary of the Queen's Awards for Export and Technological Achievement. The two pairs of se-tenant stamps were designed by Simon Broom and feature the powerful award-scheme logo. The awards – the highest honour that can be bestowed on British firms – were inaugurated in the mid-1960s at the time of tremendous new business endeavour, the ferment described by Harold Wilson as 'the white heat of technology'. Instituted by Royal Warrant in accordance

The 1990 stamps which marked the 25th anniversary of the Queen's Award for Export and Technological Achievement

with the recommendations of a committee chaired by HRH the Duke of Edinburgh, the Queen's Awards Scheme quickly established itself as a yardstick of how well British companies and organizations measured up to their challenges. Not only did the stamp dealer Stanley Gibbons receive one of these coveted awards (for exports, 1971), but the set of commemorative stamps was fittingly produced using the British-designed Quantel Paintbox graphic-design system – another winner of the award.

Also in 1990 came a five-stamp issue entitled 'Gallantry' designed by John Gibbs. This extremely handsome set featured a range of decorations including the highest award in the land for an individual – the Victoria Cross. This honour is the most senior of all British and Commonwealth awards for valour by members of the services. It was introduced in 1856 and the medals are cast from the bronze of a cannon which was captured at the Siege of Sebastopol. Fewer than 1400 people have gained the right to add VC to their name. Three of the stamps show medals depicting George VI, including of course the George Cross, which was instituted in 1940 primarily for civilians who have displayed extraordinary bravery and heroism. Showing these awards alongside the silhouette of the Queen marked the first time a British stamp had featured both the Queen and her father.

John Gibbs's elegant designs for the Gallantry issue

LION OF ENGLAND · GRIFFIN OF EDWARD III

FALCON OF PLANTAGENET · BULL OF CLARENCE

LION OF MORTIMER · YALE OF BEAUFORT

GREYHOUND OF RICHMOND · DRAGON OF WALES

UNICORN OF SCOTLAND · HORSE OF HANOVER

'The Queen's Beasts' issued in 1998 and designed by Jeffery Matthews

Towards the end of the decade came the splendid five-stamp series 'The Queen's Beasts' designed by Jeffery Matthews to celebrate the 650th anniversary of the Order of the Garter. Having been founded by Edward III, the Order of the Garter, headed by the sovereign, remains Britain's highest civil and military honour. In one of the most splendid displays of pageantry, the Garter Ceremony takes place at Windsor Castle every year on St George's Day (St George's Chapel has always been home to the Order). A vast and colourful procession weaves its way through Windsor from the Royal Apartments down the hill to the Chapel. The Queen and the Prince of Wales (who became a member in 1968) feature close to the end of the procession and are followed by the Yeoman of the Guard. After being

abandoned in 1805, this spectacular ceremony was revived in 1948 by King George VI. The heraldic theme of the stamps featured the ten Queen's beasts – part of a symbolic retinue sculpted by James Woodford – all of which stood guard as two-metre-high plaster models outside Westminster Abbey during the coronation. Portland stone versions of those same beasts now stand guard outside the Palm House at the Royal Botanic Gardens, Kew.

Windsor Castle, of course, was the scene of the terrible fire of November 1992. The castle is reputedly the Queen's favourite residence in England and, fortunately, most art treasures had been removed for renovation when the fire broke out. Prince Andrew was the only member of the royal family in the castle at the time and he immediately contacted the Queen, who rushed to Windsor from Buckingham Palace to oversee the removal of the remaining treasures. Her 'annus horribilis' speech to the Guildhall four days later was perhaps one of the most emotive speeches ever made by a member of the royal family. But more was to follow. The £60 million repair bill to Windsor Castle led to speculation in the press as to who would pay, and questioned why the Queen still was not required to pay income tax. To add to this controversy, the year ended poorly when the *Sun* newspaper obtained a copy of the Queen's Christmas broadcast and published it two days before Christmas Day – breaking the long-standing embargo agreement. Legal action brought by the Queen's lawyers led to an apology by the paper and a sizeable donation to charity.

ABOVE The Jersey stamp features a portrait of Her Majesty in Order of the Garter robes, by Norman Hepple

LEFT The Queen inspects the fire damage at Windsor Castle, 1992

LANDMARK ROYAL ANNIVERSARIES

The 1990s was studded with landmark royal anniversaries. At the start of the decade, the Queen Mother celebrated her 90th birthday, an occasion marked by a series of four stamps depicting her portrait at four stages in her life. The set was the creation of legendary designer John Gorham, and featured classic portraits by Norman Parkinson and Dorothy Wilding.

Just two years later came the 40th anniversary of the Queen's accession, an occasion which Royal Mail celebrated in style with a stamp issue entitled 'Happy and Glorious' from the words of the national anthem. The resulting stunning quintet of stamps was the work of Why Not Associates. The designers conceived the series as an interconnected, horizontal strip of images – slightly dreamlike and almost like scenes from a film – depicting five aspects of the Queen's life as Head of State, Head of the Church, Head of the Royal Family, Head of the Armed Forces and Head of Commonwealth. Each portrait – two by Cecil Beaton, one by Tim Graham and two by Anwar Hussein – was interwoven with subtle heraldic symbols and styled typography.

Lady Elizabeth Bowes-Lyon

Elizabeth Duchess of York

Queen Elizabeth

Queen Elizabeth The Queen Mother

TOP **Kenya stamp celebrating the 40th anniversary of the accession**

ABOVE **John Gorham's superb designs for the Queen Mother's 90th birthday**

For the accession anniversary the Queen again allowed TV cameras access to her life. The media focus of the 1980s had focused on her family, especially the younger members. The BBC documentary *Elizabeth R* returned attention

to the monarch and her working life. For a year a TV crew was allowed unprecedented access to the Queen with echoes of the 1969 landmark film *Royal Family*. In the 1960s the family was generally perceived as remote and the earlier film played its part in the de-mystification of the monarchy. By contrast, in 1992 it could be argued that too much demystification by the media and its scrutiny of every action had made royalty all too real. *Elizabeth R* was broadcast in the UK on Accession Day, 6 February, and was the most watched TV programme of the week. To illustrate the continuing fascination with the British monarchy abroad, the programme was subsequently shown in over 25 countries around the world.

In November 1997 came the Golden Wedding anniversary of the Queen and Prince Philip. This occasion was marked in stamps with an original

monochrome wedding photograph by society photographer Baron, alongside a contemporary colour photograph of the royal couple by the former Baron employee, Lord Snowdon. A photoshoot was organized at the Palace and the royal couple posed in formal dress as well as in very informal attire. In the event, the more formal image was selected for the stamp issue, and co-ordinated perfectly with the Baron image of 50 years earlier.

Snowdon's considerable portfolio of royal portraiture began to be assembled in the 1950s when early photographs included the royal family at

ABOVE **The 1947 wedding portrait by Baron of the Queen and Prince Philip inspired the design for their Golden Wedding stamps in 1997, which featured a photograph by Lord Snowdon**

ease in Buckingham Palace. His style of capturing the moment introduced a more naturalistic style to portraiture of the family. His marriage in 1960 to the Queen's sister, Princess Margaret, only cemented an existing close relationship to the family.

During the summer, the Queen and Prince Philip held a garden party at Buckingham Palace to which they invited couples from around the country who were also celebrating their golden weddings. And in November, for the anniversary itself, they attended a service of thanksgiving at Westminster Abbey followed by a lunch hosted by the Government at the Banqueting House. In the evening a private ball was held in the newly restored state rooms at Windsor Castle following completion of restoration work after the 1992 fire.

BELOW An informal portrait of the Queen and Prince Philip by Lord Snowdon from the Golden Wedding shoot

BELOW RIGHT One of the 'omnibus' designs celebrating the Golden Wedding

NINETIES' WEDDINGS

St George's Chapel Windsor

Perhaps the one high point of the Queen's 'annus horribilis' of 1992 was the December re-marriage of the Princess Royal. The Princess's wish for a small family affair, with the media kept at a distance was met, although this did not stop several newspapers from contrasting this with the televised pomp of her first marriage in 1973. Commentators noted how much had changed for the royal family in two decades.

The 1990s closed, however, with a thoroughly modern marriage. The youngest of the Queen and Duke of Edinburgh's children, Prince Edward, announced his engagement to Sophie Rhys-Jones right at the start of 1999. The wedding date was set for the summer. Theirs was a relatively informal wedding – more of a family occasion than a state one.

Prince Edward was born in March 1964, and after a brief spell in the Royal Marines he opted for a career in the theatre and in 1987 joined Andrew Lloyd Webber's Really Useful Company. He continued his career in the media by setting up his own television production company.

The marriage of Prince Edward and Sophie Rhys-Jones took place on 19 June 1999 in the magnificent setting of St George's Chapel, Windsor. On the same day the Queen conferred the Earldom of Wessex and the Viscountcy of Severn on Prince Edward – his wife became the Countess of Wessex – titles which had lain dormant for almost 1000 years. Thousands of well-wishers thronged the Windsor streets, and millions more around the world watched the event on TV. The pair of stamps celebrating the occasion were exactly in tune with the wishes of the royal couple for an informal celebration. The striking black and white photographs taken by John Swannell showed the bride and groom both wearing black roll-neck jumpers – happy and smiling and with no trace of royal adornment – and highlighting their closeness. The images were taken at Windsor Castle shortly after the announcement of the wedding date.

THE PAINTING PRINCE

Despite the furore of media interest in his personal life, Prince Charles has established a reputation as a dutiful and sensitive person with a real concern for disadvantaged people – particularly the young. He has also emerged as an accomplished watercolourist and a passionate advocate of careful stewardship of the land and of organic farming. As an artist he has exhibited at the Royal Academy of Arts Summer exhibition under the name of A.G. Carrick. His own farming experiments and work on the gardens at his Highgrove Estate in Gloucestershire have attracted much public attention and the Prince has occasionally been lampooned for a chance remark he once made about 'talking' to his plants to encourage them to grow.

But during the 1990s his charity work and his love of nature converged when the Prince used his skill in painting watercolours to raise funds for The Prince of Wales Charities Trust. In 1994, the 25th anniversary of his Investiture, Royal Mail sponsored a touring exhibition of the Prince's recent paintings and five attractive landscapes of Wales, Scotland, Northern Ireland and England were reproduced as Special Stamps. The paintings were an illustration not just of the Prince's enjoyment of nature but of his view that 'if we are to preserve the essential elements of this beauty and delight... man-made structures and landscaping features must be fitted in to the overall picture with sensitivity and vision' – a plea for the thoughtful conservation of the British landscape.

The Prince's developing environmental awareness was in tune with international thinking about the planet. In 1992 the United Nations

RIGHT **Paintings by Prince Charles adorned the stamps which commemorated the 25th anniversary of his investiture**

1969 1994

HRH THE PRINCE

AN EXHIBITION OF WATERCO

THE 25TH ANNIVERSARY OF I

BUCKINGHAM PALACE LONDON

Conference on the Environment and Development was held in Rio de Janeiro. It focused world attention on the dangers of plundering the earth's resources, of pollution and of global warming. More than ever people became conscious of the fragility and beauty of nature. Young people took the green cause very much to heart, which is why the choice of children's paintings for the 'Protecting the Environment' stamps of 1992 was especially apt. More than a third of all the stamps in the Millennium series of 2000 were environmentally themed (see page 98), and a series celebrating success in reversing the decline of species began with an issue on birds in 2007.

Castell Y Waun / Chirk Castle, Clwyd, Cymru / Wales

Ben Arkle, Sutherland, Scotland

Mourne Mountains, County Down, Northern Ireland

Dersingham, Norfolk, England

Dolwyddelan, Gwynedd, Cymru / Wales

I MARCH 1994 LONDON SW1A1AA BUCKINGHAM PALACE

ROYAL ART

The Royal Collection is a vast assemblage of works of art in all forms, including around 7000 paintings as well as other artworks such as furniture and ceramics. It is the only one of the world's great royal collections to have retained a degree of independence. The greater part of

FINO AND TINY
GEORGE STUBBS

the collection is Crown property, held in trust for the nation by the sovereign, although there are some artworks which are the property of Her Majesty. The Queen and the Duke of Edinburgh own a number of pictures by Commonwealth artists which have been purchased or commissioned. The

A ROUGH DOG
GEORGE STUBBS

Queen, in particular, has acquired paintings by post war British artists including L.S. Lowry and Graham Sutherland. A number of images from the Royal Collection have appeared on stamps such as the dog paintings by Stubbs, in 1991. Contrast these with the contemp-

orary watercolours of cats created by Elizabeth Blackadder RA RSA for the 1995 stamps. Blackadder was appointed Her Majesty's Painter and Limner in Scotland in 2001.

NO LONGER AN ISLAND NATION

The realization of the European Community in 1992 was greeted by an ebullient stamp image by one of Britain's finest artists, David Hockney – a dancing European star. Perhaps the feeling of connection to the Continent did not become wholly real to many people until the completion of the Channel tunnel two years later. In 1994 the opening of the tunnel made the dream of a ground link between Britain and Continental Europe a reality for the first time since the Ice Age. Europe's biggest infrastructure project involved 13,000 engineers and the digging of 95 miles of tunnels 150 feet under the seabed. The link was designed not simply as one tunnel but three – one for trains in each direction plus a service tunnel.

Far from the Victorian idea of steam trains running through a gas-lit tube, the modern tunnel was provided with high-speed trains to bring England and France together in an unprecedented way. And it was together that the Queen and President Mitterand opened the Channel Tunnel. No longer an isolated island, the symbolism of Britain's new relationship with her closest neighbour and old ally was lost on no one. Appropriately the event was marked by a joint Anglo-French stamp issue – a pair designed by George Hardie and Jean-Paul Cousin – one showing the British lion and French cockerel joined in an arch over the tunnel, the other showing symbolic hands over a train. Stamps similar in design were issued in France.

The mid-1990s were, in another way, a time for remembering Britain's old alliance with France. The liberation of Europe, which started with D-Day in 1944, was commemorated in a series of moving events and a set of Special Stamps which recalled images seen in news journals – most notably the

renowned *Picture Post* – of the 1940s. The Queen attended commemorative services at the Bayeux war cemetery and Omaha beach in Normandy, France. In the following year, VE and VJ Day 50th-anniversary celebrations culminated in

a memorable ceremony of peace and reconciliation in Hyde Park in May. In August, at the Royal Victoria Memorial, a gathering of war veterans observed a two-minute silence as a Lancaster bomber showered more than a million poppies onto the assembled crowds. That evening the Queen

and the Duke of Edinburgh sailed down the Thames to board the Royal Yacht *Britannia* and the skies lit up to a fly-past and firework display from five bridges to celebrate the anniversary of the end of the war.

A NATION IN MOURNING – THE DEATH OF DIANA

Millions of people around the world remember what they were doing when they heard the news of the death of Diana, Princess of Wales. The days that followed the fatal car crash in Paris on the last day of August 1997 were some of the most extraordinary and emotional that Britain had experienced since the Second World War. There was a nationwide, spontaneous outpouring of grief as Diana's body was returned to London and lay privately at the Chapel Royal at St James's Palace. Around the country people queued for hours in respectful silence to sign books of condolence. Millions of flowers were laid by mourners at the royal palaces. Kensington Palace, the former home of the Princess, became a place of vigil. Many of the mourners expressed the feeling that they had lost not just a much-loved public figure but a friend; they valued Diana's talent for empathy with ordinary people and her charity work with children and the sick. Diana's life may have been troubled but her popularity was astonishing. The funeral itself – free from pomp and regalia – was a fitting ceremony for the 'People's Princess' and the mother of two dearly loved sons.

Clearly Diana had changed the image of the royal family for ever. Not only did she increase the glamour associated with royalty, but she played her part in championing charitable causes and breaking down taboos such as those surrounding AIDS sufferers.

From the moment the tragedy was announced it was clear that Royal Mail would be expected to respond with a special tribute stamp issue. It was decided to use photographs which depicted the main aspects of her character – the compassionate, humanitarian, charity figure and the glamorous princess. Though the stamps – created by Royal Mail's Design Director, Barry Robinson – were ready for printing within two weeks of the Princess's death, there were legal formalities to complete. This meant that the five stamps did not finally go on sale until February 1998. On the morning of issue Britain's post offices were besieged by people wanting to buy the stamps. As a final honour to the memory of Diana, Royal Mail donated more than £9 million from the sale of the stamps to the Princess's Memorial Fund.

OPPOSITE: **Photograph by Lord Snowdon**

LEFT (CLOCKWISE FROM TOP LEFT): **Photographs by John Stillwell, Lord Snowdon, Terence Donovan, Tim Graham**

A New
Century

2000ˢ

'As we come together and look forward to the coming year, I hope that we shall be able to find ways of strengthening our own communities as a sure support and comfort – whatever may lie ahead.'

THE QUEEN'S CHRISTMAS
MESSAGE, DECEMBER 2001

27

TIMELINE

2000

The Queen led celebrations of the arrival of the year 2000 at the Millennium Dome

State visits to Australia and Italy

Nelson Mandela was received by the Queen and the Duke of Edinburgh

2001

State visit to Norway

The President of the Republic of South Africa and Mrs Mbeki received at Windsor Castle

US President George Bush met the Queen at Buckingham Palace

State visit to the Queen and the Duke of Edinburgh by the King and Queen of Jordan

2002

Deaths of Princess Margaret and Queen Elizabeth, the Queen Mother

Visits to Jamaica, New Zealand, Australia and Canada

The Queen made an historic address to both Houses of Parliament

The Queen opened the new Queen's Gallery at Buckingham Palace

National holiday in June for the Golden Jubilee

2003

Celebration of the 50th anniversary of the coronation

President Putin's state visit to the UK, the first by a Russian leader in 129 years

The President of the USA and Mrs Bush welcomed by the Queen at a ceremony outside Buckingham Palace

The Queen and the Duke of Edinburgh arrived in Nigeria to attend the Commonwealth Heads of Government Meeting

2004

State visit to France

The President of the Republic of Poland arrived at Buckingham Palace on a state visit to the Queen

The Queen accompanied by the Duke of Edinburgh, opened the new Stock Exchange building in Paternoster Square, London

The President of the Republic of Hungary and Mrs Mádl visited the Queen

The President of the French Republic visits the Queen and the Duke of Edinburgh to mark the Centenary of The Entente Cordiale

2005

State visit by the President of the Italian Republic

The Queen unveiled the National Police Memorial on Cambridge Green, The Mall, London

Visit to Canada (Saskatchewan and Alberta)

The Queen undertook engagements in Dover/Portsmouth to recognise Britain's maritime heritage

The Queen and the Duke of Edinburgh attended a Service in St Paul's Cathedral to commemorate the 60th Anniversary of the United Nations

The Queen and the Duke of Edinburgh attended a Service of Remembrance for the London Bombings, 2005, in St Paul's Cathedral, London

The Queen and the Duke of Edinburgh visit Malta, attending the Commonwealth Heads of Government Meeting

2006

The Queen and the Duke of Edinburgh visit Australia and Singapore

State visit by the President of Brazil to the Queen and the Duke of Edinburgh

The Queen attended a service of thanksgiving in St George's Chapel, Windsor Castle, for Her Majesty's 80th birthday

The Queen, Patron, Victoria Cross and George Cross Association, gave a reception at Windsor Castle to mark its 150th anniversary

The Queen hosted a party for 2000 children at Buckingham Palace

State Visits to Lithuania, Latvia and Estonia (The Baltic States)

The Queen and the Duke of Edinburgh gave a reception at Buckingham Palace to recognise the work of the Duke of Edinburgh's Award

2007

State visit to the USA by the Queen and the Duke of Edinburgh. Visited Virginia to mark the 400th Anniversary of the Jamestown settlement

The Queen opened the new planetarium at the Royal Observatory, Greenwich

The Queen and the Duke of Edinburgh visit Romsey, Hampshire to mark the 400th Anniversary of the Royal Charter

The Queen and the Duke of Edinburgh celebrate their Diamond Wedding Anniversary

THE 2000s

The excitement and anticipation which surrounded the approaching new millennium was marked by a massive public building boom around the British Isles. In just about every major town and city, new bridges, museums, galleries and visitor attractions were created as a mark of optimism for the new age. Some – such as Cornwall's Eden Project – were an instant and huge hit with visitors and critics, while others – such as the Dome in Greenwich, London – had a more troubled history. Both, however, succeeded as an engine for local regeneration. While this work was underway, other major new developments included the opening of the Scottish Parliament and the Welsh Assembly. And the Northern Ireland peace process matured as the route to power sharing in the province was consolidated.

Early in the decade, celebrations for the Queen's Golden Jubilee were mingled with great sadness at the deaths of the Queen Mother and Princess Margaret. Meanwhile, the newest generation of royals matured as princes William and Harry both passed 21. Prince William completed his university studies at St Andrews and the brothers trained to become army officers.

For many people, the new millennium began on 11 September 2001 when the world was shaken by history's most horrific terrorist attack. The subsequent actions in Iraq and Afghanistan and the terrible London bombings of July 2005 were the counterpoint to the optimism of the celebrations that began the decade.

Against the changing and uncertain backdrop, institutions like the monarchy provided a sense of continuity and stability. Royal visits, concerts, services of thanksgiving and countrywide pageants marked significant anniversaries including the Golden Jubilee and the very heartfelt celebrations of the Queen's 80th birthday. In her ninth decade, the Queen remains a unifying figure for the nation.

MARKING THE MILLENNIUM

To mark the Millennium, Royal Mail issued its most extensive and ambitious stamp programme by far. The scheme spanned 1999 and 2000 and comprised 100 special stamps issued over 25 months. The 1999 project celebrated 'the past', and intensive research located 48 iconic endeavours or events to encapsulate 1000 years of British history. Some 48 diverse image-makers were invited to bring their creative talents to bear on the 48 subjects. This unprecedented exercise of commissioning and organization was ordered into twelve monthly 'Tales'

Designs from the ambitious Millennium stamps programme of 1999, including a Dalek photographed by Lord Snowdon

exploring keynotes in history. The cycle began with the Inventors' Tale, followed by the Travellers' Tale and continued through the year concluding with the Artists' Tale. Each image-maker – including painters, photographers, a weaver, wood and lino-cut artists and even a silversmith – was carefully paired with a topic that had a particular resonance with his or her work.

The start of the 1999 series was marked by an exquisite design, the 99th stamp by artist David Gentleman. Appropriately the theme was timekeeping, and the elegant illustrated image incorporated a clock face, the turning world and a red line to mark the Greenwich Meridian. The second stamp – also part of the Inventor's Tale and on the theme of steam power – by artist Peter Howson, drew comments in the press when it was pointed out that the Queen's head was 'going up in a puff of smoke' belching from a factory chimney. Later in the year stamps by, among others, Don McCullin, Bridget Riley and Peter Blake were issued, as well as Lord Snowdon's portrait of TV Doctor Who's arch adversary, a dalek.

The second series, which spanned 2000, had an entirely different flavour. This next 'super set' of 48 stamps was a celebration of 'the present' in the form of the spirit of 48 of the many cultural and architectural celebrations marking the millennium. Tellingly, the stamps were all photographic images. Among them were some of the great new endeavours including the Dynamic Earth Centre in Edinburgh, The Lowry in Salford, Tate Modern in London, the Gateshead Millennium Bridge and performers at the Dome – some of which were officially opened by the Queen.

The series culminated with a final set of four stamps in January 2001 to focus on 'the future'. Appropriately, these images were photographs of four face-painted children, inspired by the UN Convention on the Rights of the Child, and in particular celebrating the next generation – today's physical embodiment of the future (right).

Remarkably, more than two billion stamps were printed in the Millennium series – laid side by side they would provide enough gummed paper to circle the Earth twice. A specially re-cropped image of the Machin portrait of the Queen on a clean white background was also created for the year 2000.

DAVID GENTLEMAN

Having designed more than 100 stamps, artist David Gentleman is Britain's best known and most prolific designer of stamps. And along with his consistently inspiring and brilliant output he also played a pivotal role in the evolution of modern stamp design.

Born in 1930, he studied at St Alban's School of Art followed by the Royal College of Art. Gentleman first became involved in stamp design in 1962 when he was commissioned to design a trio of stamps to celebrate National Productivity Year. The series features powerful graphics, but it is clear that the finished product suffered from the rather uninspiring subject matter and the requirement to include a large portrait of the Queen. Despite the drawbacks, the work was clearly considered a success since it was David Gentleman who was called upon to complete the hastily produced stamps to mark the death of Winston Churchill in 1965. This was swiftly followed by the controversial, but graphically brilliant series to mark the 25th anniversary of the Battle of Britain. The controversy was sparked by the depiction of a German swastika on one of the stamps. Gentleman recollects the incident, which even provoked debate in the House of Commons: 'There was a fuss about the German insignia on the planes in my Battle of Britain set. The Foreign Office said they would harm Anglo-German relations. Tony Benn, then Postmaster General, said that this was nonsense – battles were about adversaries, not friendly relations – and the swastikas and Iron Crosses stayed on the stamps.'

In addition to his contribution as one of the country's greatest designers of individual stamps, Gentleman is also credited with actually inspiring the concept of modern pictorial stamp design. Through his landmark album of the mid-1960s, commissioned by Postmaster General Tony Benn, he suggested a way forward for contemporary designs which would produce exciting and stimulating imagery. He also developed new ways of incorporating the sovereign's head within the design so that it might sit more comfortably with the main image of the stamp.

Throughout his decades of working with Royal Mail, David Gentleman has pursued a highly varied career working on diverse projects such as advertising and award-winning posters for the likes of the National Trust and London Underground, and the platform-long murals at London's Charing Cross underground station. His epic series of travel albums have taken him to India, Italy, France and beyond.

18

Among his many stamp design triumphs, the most recent were for the Royal Mail Millennium Stamps project. Gentleman was chosen by Royal Mail to begin the 1999 project with his 99th issued stamp design. Entitled 'Timekeeping', the stamps were a salute to John Harrison's chronometer and the Greenwich Meridian, and the memorable design features a globe, a clock face and the red line of the Zero Meridian. The elements are combined to link the idea of the turning world and the passage of time – as ever, an elegant solution to a challenging brief – and best appreciated by viewing a sheet of stamps (below). To usher in the public celebrations at the very end of 1999, Gentleman was commissioned to reprise his design in a miniature sheet of four stamps.

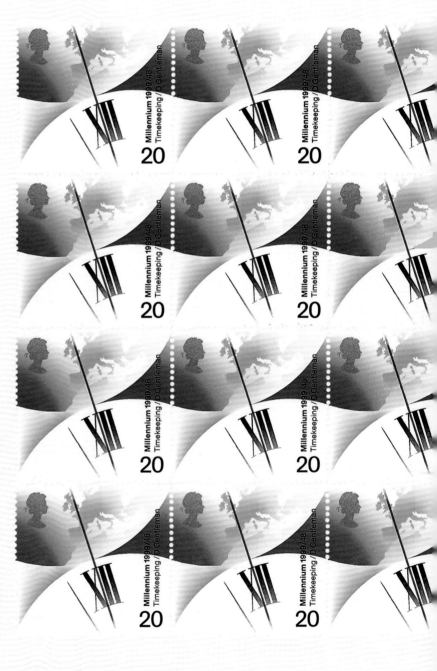

THE QUEEN MOTHER AT 100

Her Majesty Queen Elizabeth the Queen Mother is regarded with enormous affection by the British public and the occasion of her 100th birthday in August 2000 was a tremendous moment for celebration.

Born at the turn of the 20th century – during the very last months of the reign of Queen Victoria – Elizabeth Bowes-Lyon grew up in Hertfordshire, at Glamis Castle in Scotland and Streatham Castle, County Durham. When she was aged 14, Britain declared war on Germany; her brother Fergus was killed, two other brothers were wounded and a fourth was taken prisoner. In 1923 her

life took a happier turn when she married Prince Albert, Duke of York. As Duchess of York she gave birth to her first daughter, Elizabeth, in 1926 and, four years later, a second daughter, Margaret Rose.

Life for the family appeared to be mapped out on a steady course with the two young daughters growing up in a formal family with its aristocratic background. However, events took a dramatic turn in December 1936 with the startling news of the abdication of Edward VIII, who was forced to choose between duty to his country and love for Mrs Wallis Warfield Simpson – an American divorcee. Next in line to the throne was Edward's brother, the Duke of York, who became King George VI – making his wife, the Duchess of York, Queen Consort and Empress at the age of 36.

At the outbreak of the Second World War the royal family, including the two young princesses, took the courageous decision to stay in London. Like thousands of other homes in the capital, Buckingham Palace was bombed and this shared experience in adversity proved a powerful bond between the royal family and its subjects. Frequently the King and Queen toured the bombed ruins in London and the rest of Britain and the Queen's reassuring radio broadcasts won a huge and appreciative audience.

Her debut on stamps was made on the occasion of the King's coronation in 1937 and was followed in 1948 with stamps issued to celebrate the Royal Silver Wedding. Following the death of her husband and accession of her daughter,

Queen Elizabeth the Queen Mother stepped back out of the limelight. This allowed her to pursue interests in gardening, fishing and dogs – it was the Queen Mother who introduced the corgi into the royal household – and of course, her passionate interest in horse racing. Nevertheless, her round of royal engagements has continued well past her 100th year and she continues as patron or president of more than 350 organisations including churches, hospitals, charities and

The miniature sheet of four stamps issued to celebrate the Queen Mother's 100th birthday

societies. For 25 years she was Chancellor of the University of London and she became the first woman to be appointed Lord Warden of the Cinque Ports. She is Colonel-in-Chief of several military regiments and Commandant-in-Chief of all the women's services.

To celebrate her 100th birthday a highly unusual set of stamps was issued. The design was based on a portrait photograph by John Swannell, which was actually taken on the Queen Mother's 99th birthday, showing four generations of the royal family. Swannell and his subjects were themselves filmed during the photographic session and made an appearance in the Queen's Christmas broadcast of 1999. The completed stamps feature as part of a tableau showing the Queen Mother surrounded by the Queen, Prince Charles and Prince William, in his first appearance on a UK stamp.

To complement the 'visual laureate' role of British stamps to mark royal occasions, Royal Mail commissioned Poet Laureate Andrew Motion to compose a poem to mark the Queen Mother's birthday, which explored the notion of recollection and images encapsulated in portraits and photography.

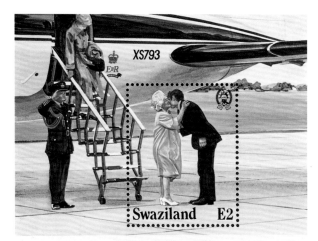

XS793

The Life and Times of Her Majesty Queen Elizabeth The Queen Mother

Swaziland E2

Exploring and reinventing the traditions of royal portraiture is not confined to stamps, of course. Contrast the 'stamp-size' photography of John Swannell with the similarly inspired but 12-foot high oil painting by John Wonnacott. It was the artist's suggestion that the Queen Mother's centenary might be an appropriate occasion for the National Portrait Gallery to commission a portrait of the royal lineage. The resulting painting featuring six members of the family, and four corgis (belonging to the Queen Mother) is striking in its wide-angle informality in the white and gold room of Buckingham Palace. The vigour and youth of Prince William in the foreground contrasts with the elegance of the 100-year-old great-grandmother. A family is presented – at once both ordinary and extraordinary. The kind of family who regularly appear on postage stamps.

ABOVE **A decorative stamp from Swaziland celebrating the life of the Queen Mother**

RIGHT **The Queen Mother enjoys her birthday surrounded by her family**

THE MONARCHS' STAMPS

The superb Royal Philatelic Collection is one of the most comprehensive collections of stamps in the world. It was originally begun in 1864 by Prince Alfred, Queen Victoria's second son. The Queen is the fifth monarch to inherit it, following George VI (right), and it now runs to more than 300 albums and some 200 boxes, stored in vaults at St James's Palace. Her recent contribution to upgrade the collection was the sale at auction of 'duplicate' items and purchase of a unique set of ten Penny Blacks. The gem of the collection is a Mauritian stamp valued at £2 million, which went on show in a Golden Jubilee travelling exhibition in 2002 along with other stamp treasures from the royal collection.

A DEPICTION OF IDENTITY

With the incoming Labour Government of 1997 came an intense period of debate on national identity. What was 'New Britain'? What, indeed was 'Britishness'? The referendum on, and then establishment of, a separate Parliament for Scotland and Assembly for Wales, plus progress in Northern Ireland and the re-establishment of government at Stormont, provided much scope for debate and reflection in the Queen's realm. To commemorate the landmark devolution for Scotland and Wales, new definitive stamp designs for these countries were developed.

Definitives for Scotland, Wales and Northern Ireland had existed in varying forms since 1958, but devolution presented great design challenges for Royal Mail. Encapsulating a sense of 'nationhood' in a minute space (less than half an inch square) which also features a monetary value as well as the profile of the Queen, is a hard enough job, but the visual imagery had to be iconic enough to say 'Scotland' or 'Wales' in its own right. Design groups in the respective countries were commissioned to develop proposals: Scotland and Wales for 1999, followed by designs for Northern Ireland and England in 2001. These four sets are united in their diversity – a telling metaphor, perhaps, for how the constituent parts of the UK connect. The Welsh stamps, for example, included a leek carved from Welsh sycamore, a dragon crafted from Welsh steel and the Prince of Wales' feathers fashioned from Welsh gold and silver. The year 2001 also marked the 200th anniversary of the present design of the Union Flag. A Special Stamp was issued to commemorate this event: a crisp flag designed by Dick Davis.

TOP ROW **English definitive stamps**

BOTTOM LEFT QUARTET **Definitives for Northern Island**

BOTTOM RIGHT QUARTET **Scottish definitive stamps**

THE GOLDEN JUBILEE

Celebrating a remarkable half-century as monarch, the Queen's Golden Jubilee year of 2002 provided an occasion not only to look back at her role in the affairs of the United Kingdom and the Commonwealth, but also to look to the future. Six key themes were identified for the Jubilee. The first was 'Celebration', and the opportunity for the whole nation and Commonwealth to unite in a weekend of special events in June – a focus was provided by the National Service of Thanksgiving at St Paul's Cathedral on 4 June. The second theme was 'Giving Thanks'; through tours and visits during 2002 the Queen took the opportunity to express her thanks for continued support and loyalty. 'Service' was the third theme – a time to acknowledge all those who support

The Golden Jubilee stamps, issued on 6 February 2002

and contribute to their communities. The fourth was 'Involving the Whole Community'; a series of celebrations were held nationwide to reflect the multicultural and diverse members of today's society. The fifth theme was 'Looking Forward as Well as Back' – time to both reflect on the changes of the previous half-century and also celebrate the achievements of young people, the next generation. Finally, the theme of 'Commonwealth' explored the modern significance of this historic group of nations. The Queen opened the

XVII Commonwealth Games in Manchester, and the 'friendly games' were celebrated in a stamp issue in July.

To mark the landmark anniversary of the accession, Royal Mail issued a simple and elegant quintet of stamps, each featuring a close-cropped portrait of the Queen and charting the decades of her reign. The medium of black-and-white photography was chosen by designer Kate Stephens. The simplicity of the monochrome images – by such important photographers as Dorothy Wildling, Cecil Beaton, Lord Snowdon, Yousef Karsh and Tim Graham – adds poignancy to the portraits, as well as reflecting on previous stamps featuring their work. The Queen is shown free of the impressive regalia

of her position; there is no crown, no ermine cloak, no retinue, no display of pomp or power. This collection of images stands then in stark contrast to the royal portraiture of the past – Kate Stephens was also designer of the impressive Henry VIII issue of 1997. The smiling, open face of the Queen in the third millennium could hardly be further from those imposing portraits of Henry VIII or indeed the Gloriana-style of depiction chosen by the coolly controlling first Elizabeth.

The year of Golden Jubilee celebrations included the Queen making visits to Jamaica, New Zealand, Australia and Canada, a tour of 70 British cities and towns and a national weekend of celebrations. While cynics predicted there would be a lack of interest, the participation of millions of citizens proved them entirely wrong.

The Jubilee weekend at the beginning of June was thoroughly enjoyed around the country with hundreds of street parties and local events. Meanwhile, the high points were two concerts which took place in the garden at Buckingham Palace. Some 24,000 members of the public attended the twin events having won tickets in a ballot (some 2 million applied). The line-up at Saturday's classical concert included Dame Kiri Te Kanawa, Sir Thomas Allen and Mstislav Rostropovich with the BBC Symphony Orchestra and chorus conducted by Sir Andrew Davis, while Monday's pop concert kicked off in spectacular style with guitarist Brian May of rock group Queen on the roof of Buckingham Palace playing a solo rendition of the national anthem. Millions of TV viewers saw performers celebrating 50 years of British music: from Cliff Richard and Tom Jones to Ozzy Osbourne. Sir Paul McCartney appeared for the show's closing songs which concluded in a grand finale with the event's stars on stage singing 'All You Need is Love'. Earlier in the day a mass singing of this Beatles' classic took place throughout the UK. Following the music, the Queen lit a beacon outside Buckingham Palace to begin a spectacular fireworks display and also to signal the start of a chain of 1700 beacons lit across the Commonwealth. A memorable day of festivities and parades on Tuesday concluded the extended bank holiday Jubilee weekend.

Prince Charles addresses the audience of the concert with the Queen and pop royalty on stage. Stamps of The Beatles album covers were among the most popular stamps issued by Royal Mail in recent years

IN MEMORIAM

Alongside the joyous events of the Golden Jubilee year, the Queen endured great personal sorrow with the deaths of her sister and mother.

On 9 February 2002 The Princess Margaret, Countess of Snowdon, died peacefully in her sleep at The King Edward VII Hospital in London. Aged 71, she had suffered poor health for some years. The funeral took place in St George's Chapel, Windsor, and was a private affair attended by family and friends.

The following month, on 30 March and aged 101, Her Majesty Queen Elizabeth The Queen Mother died at Royal Lodge, Windsor. The great sadness at her death was tempered by the knowledge that she had lived a long and full life. Born while Queen Victoria was still on the throne, the Queen Mum had witnessed extraordinary change in her lifetime including world wars, man landing on the Moon and the growth of modern Britain.

The Queen Mother lay in state for three days at Westminster Hall where her four grandsons, the princes Charles, Andrew and Edward along with Viscount Linley,

mounted a vigil at the corners of her coffin on the evening before the funeral. An estimated 200,000 members of the public filed past to pay their respects, some having waited for up to six hours in queues almost three miles long. On 9 April more than a million people lined the funeral route and the sombre and dignified service took place at Westminster Abbey. It was followed by a committal service at St George's Chapel, Windsor, where her body was interred beside her husband King George VI. At the same time Princess Margaret's casket was interred with her mother and father.

The occasion was marked with a series of portrait stamps reissued from the Queen Mother's 90th birthday celebrations. They were given the addition of a black border bearing her name and the dates of her birth and death. Created by ever-popular designer John Gorham, who died in 2001, they stand as a tribute to his work too.

The 50th anniversary of the Coronation was marked on 2 June 2003. Unlike the day in 1953 which was cold and windy, the anniversary was warm and sunny. The formalities began with a thanksgiving service at Westminster Abbey with members of the royal family and more than 2000 guests. The list of people attending included more than 200 people who witnessed the original ceremony, 34 Coronation-day babies celebrating their 50th birthdays and 1000 members of the public selected from a ticket ballot. Also present was Everest climber Sir Edmund Hillary whose news of reaching the mountain's summit hit the headlines on Coronation day in 1953. (The 50th anniversary of this momentous endeavour was commemorated in a stamp in April.)

Following the service the Queen and Prince Philip were driven to The Mall where the Queen unveiled a plaque to commemorate the extension of the Jubilee Walkway. On to Buckingham Palace and the Queen presented the first Golden Jubilee Awards for voluntary service.

During the afternoon 500 children attended a tea party in Buckingham Palace gardens which was transformed by carousels, entertainers and a circus tent into a giant playground. The children attending were drawn from three organizations: Barnardo's, The London Taxi Drivers' Fund for Underprivileged Children and SSAFA, an organization supporting the families of servicemen and women. The Queen took part in a walkabout at the end of the afternoon and cut a special Coronation cake. A private party concluded the day.

The occasion was marked by a set of ten stamps, five recalling the Coronation with evocative scenes of the Queen's subjects, and five were of the formal occasion. To distinguish between the parallel stories, the public celebrations were shown in black-and-white, while the formal photos were in colour. Among the memorable images was the classic Cecil Beaton portrait of the Queen and a rare colour shot from the day of the gold State Coach.

The Coronation anniversary stamps designed by Kate Stephens, with the Everest commemoration (above), also from 2003

PRINCE WILLIAM COMES OF AGE

Prince William, second in line to the throne, and with dashing good looks, celebrated his 21st birthday on 21 June 2003. He was christened Prince William Arthur Philip Louis Windsor and despite intense media and public interest in the young prince, his parents made it clear from the start that they wanted William and his brother Harry to try and enjoy childhoods that were as normal as possible.

Aged three, Prince William attended a nursery school in West London, followed by Wetherby School, also in West London, where both his parents took part in races on the school's sports day. As an eight-year-old he started at Ludgrove School in Berkshire where his flair for sports including rugby, hockey, swimming and football was encouraged.

After attending Eton College where among many other achievements he became the fastest junior swimmer in a decade and captained the swimming team, Prince William took a gap year before going on to study History of Art at St Andrews University in Scotland. Like many students, during his year out the Prince took the opportunity to travel. He took part in survival exercises with the Welsh Guards in Belize, enjoyed a safari in Africa and worked as a volunteer in a Raleigh International community project in Chile. He also relished time spent as a labourer on a British dairy farm.

While during his early life he avoided media attention, Prince William was thrust into the spotlight in 1997 at the death of his mother, Diana, Princess of Wales. Although only 15 years old, his courage at that time helped to endear him to the nation. Indeed, like his mother, he has acquired a worldwide fan club.

Since his coming of age, Prince William has graduated from university and trained as an army officer at the Royal Military Academy Sandhurst. Now in the Household Cavalry, he has also started to play an active role in public life, including representing the Queen in New Zealand to commemorate the 50th anniversary of the end of the Second World War, becoming patron of the homelessness charity Centrepoint, and patron of The Football Association.

Prince William became the first member of the royal family to have stamps issued to celebrate a 21st birthday. The four stamps, closely cropped and contemporary in feel, were designed by Madeleine Bennett.

Prince William is greeted by his grandmother at his graduation at St Andrews

THE WEDDING OF CHARLES AND CAMILLA

In a simple civil ceremony at Windsor on 9 April 2005, HRH The Prince of Wales was married to Camilla Rosemary Parker Bowles (née Shand). On her marriage, marked with a ring of Welsh gold, Mrs Parker Bowles became HRH The Duchess of Cornwall and the most senior female member of the royal family after the Queen. Along with supporting the work of her husband, the Duchess has interests in a wide variety of charities, among them the National Osteoporosis Society, of which she is president, and the British Equestrian Foundation of which she is patron. She became president of Barnardo's in 2007.

More than 20,000 well-wishers cheered as the couple arrived at Windsor's Guildhall for their small private civil wedding. Afterwards, at St George's Chapel in Windsor Castle, a service of blessing was led by the Archbishop of Canterbury. Around 800 of the couple's family and friends attended including the Queen and Prince Philip. Political figures, diplomats, church leaders and showbusiness personalities were among the congregation.

Camilla's great grandmother Alice Keppel with her daughter

The Duchess drew praise for her sense of style. She wore an oyster silk basket-weave coat and chiffon dress for the civil ceremony, then changed into a porcelain blue silk dress for the marriage blessing. Philip Treacy designed her hat, which was natural straw overlaid with ivory French lace and trimmed with feathers. After the ceremony, the couple talked to members of the public outside the chapel and enjoyed a reception hosted by the Queen at the castle's State Apartments.

Following the reception, the newly-wed couple departed for their honeymoon at Birkhall on the edge of the Balmoral Estate in Scotland. Princes William and Harry had decorated the Bentley which drove the couple away from the castle.

Stamps for the occasion featured photographs of the couple, one showing them in profile at the Mey Highland Games, the other depicting them at Balmoral. The issue was produced in record time to ensure it appeared on the day of the wedding. Camilla is not the first in her family to appear on a stamp; her great-grandmother appeared on a Greetings stamp in the mid-1990s.

8 APRIL 2005
HRH THE PRINCE OF WALES AND
MRS CAMILLA PARKER BOWLES

8 EBRILL 2005
EUB TYWYSOG CYMRU A
MRS CAMILLA PARKER BOWLES

ROYAL PAGEANTRY

Artillery, provides the 41-gun royal salute after the Queen's return to Buckingham Palace and the RAF performs a fly-past.

After months of rehearsals, the action at Horse Guards Parade centres on marching in close formation and the split-second timing is watched on TV by as many as 12 million viewers worldwide. When they have completed their ceremonial duties, all soldiers return to full-time active service.

The pomp and pageantry of official ceremonies in Britain is unrivalled. And ranking among the most impressive spectacles in the calendar is Trooping the Colour. Also known as the Queen's Birthday Parade, it takes place every year to mark the Queen's official birthday in June.

The roots of this military parade can be traced back centuries, long before the establishment of the British Army. Regimental colours, or flags, were used as rallying points in battle. With only a very few exceptions, the parade has taken place almost every year since 1820.

The vast and highly complex event involves more than 1200 soldiers including more than 250 musicians and around 200 men on horseback. The soldiers are drawn

The splendour of the event was marked in 2005 with a series of six Special Stamps designed by Why Not Associates. The colourful and detailed images included an imposing image of a Scots Guard holding the ensign known as the colour on the second-class stamp; a trumpeter of the Household Cavalry on the 42p; and a detail of the uniform

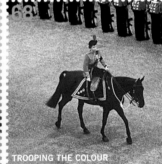

from the Household Division comprising the Grenadier, Coldstream, Scots, Irish and Welsh guards, plus the two Household Cavalry regiments of the Life Guards and the Blues and Royals. In addition, the King's Troop, Royal Horse

of the Welsh Guardsman, distinguished by features including the five buttons, on the 60p. The 68p stamp showed the Queen on Burmese, the horse she rode at the parade for many years until the mid-1980s.

ROYAL PATRONAGE

As well as being head of the armed forces and colonel in chief of the Blues and Royals, the Queen is patron of more than 620 charities and organisations. These range from the Royal Astronomical Society to the RSPCA and RSPB, Rugby Football Union as well as League, from RNIB to RIBA, from the Company of Royal Military Police to the Library Association. Dozens of these organisations have been directly celebrated on stamps over the past 50 years. Dozens more have been indirectly featured when the subjects of their activities are depicted on stamps, and they provide expert advice on the development of specific stamp issues. Here is a small selection of these philatelic tributes.

A flotilla of stamps celebrating the work of organisations which benefit from the Queen's patronage: from 1966's Westminster Abbey issue to 2008's set featuring the work of the RNLI

Always with a warm smile and quiet dignity, the Queen celebrated her 80th birthday on 21 April 2006. The occasion was marked by a sequence of events between April and the date of her official birthday in June. She received more than 20,000 birthday cards and almost as many e-mails from members of the public.

The calendar of celebrations began with a birthday reception and lunch on 19 April where almost 100 other 80-year-olds from Britain and as far away as Australia, Canada and New Zealand were invited to Buckingham Palace. Two days later, on the birthday morning, the Queen took part in a walkabout at Windsor where thousands of people turned out to offer their best wishes, wave their union flags and hand over birthday cards and bouquets. As she walked through the crowds, resplendent in bright pink, everyone joined in a hearty rendition of Happy Birthday. In the evening, a fireworks and laser display was followed by a grand family party held at the just-refurbished Kew Palace in the Royal Botanic Gardens, Kew. A birthday dedication from Prince Charles was broadcast on TV and radio.

During the following weeks, the Queen's diary included services of thanksgiving at St George's Chapel, Windsor, and at St Paul's Cathedral in London, and a special dinner at the Mansion House. Just after her official birthday, a great party attended by 2000 children was held in Buckingham Palace gardens. Among the guests were authors including J. K. Rowling, and entertainers included dozens of children's storybook characters from Noddy to Winnie the Pooh, celebrating the magic of reading.

This major celebration was also marked with a number of official birthday portraits including a photographic study by Lord Snowdon and a three-quarter length oil-painted portrait by 28-year-old artist Jemma Phipps. These joined the earlier work commissioned from Rolf Harris which had been the subject of an insightful BBC TV documentary attracting millions of viewers.

Royal Mail's stamps continued the portraiture theme with eight informal photographic images taken through the decades of the Queen's life. Designed by Sedley Place, the photographs were chosen to portray the Queen as herself,

The children's Party at the Palace was a great success… and included an appearance by a familiar postman

relaxed and smiling, away from the pressures of her official life. Among the first to be selected, and one of the most captivating, was a 1972 photograph by Lord Lichfield taken on board the Royal Yacht *Britannia*. The Queen is shown in sunglasses and a sleeveless dress enjoying the sun and smiling broadly. This image set the benchmark in the long search for seven other similarly captivating images.

THE WORKING MONARCH

Despite being in her ninth decade, the Queen's workload has shown no signs of diminishing. While there is hardly a day that could be described as typical, most mornings begin with reading newspapers, responding to as many as 300 letters, going through official papers, and holding official meetings and audiences with a range of people from overseas ambassadors to bishops and judges. There is also the presentation of honours – the Queen has conferred almost 400,000 since 1952, along with more than 540 investitures. The very first investiture of her reign was in fact one of the most profound. She conferred a Victoria Cross to Pte William Speakman just three weeks after her accession. In 2005 she conferred the VC to Pte Johnson Beharry, the first to a living recipient since 1969.

Lunchtime is often quiet and private, but there are occasional official lunches. With the administration completed, the afternoons are for public engagements. Preparation is always meticulous and the Queen is briefed on who she will meet and what she will be seeing and doing. The Queen carries

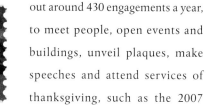

out around 430 engagements a year, to meet people, open events and buildings, unveil plaques, make speeches and attend services of thanksgiving, such as the 2007 commemoration of the Abolition of Slavery. The Duke of Edinburgh will often accompany the Queen on visits; they will carry out some engagements jointly and others separately to ensure visits to the maximum number of people.

Official occasions in which the Queen led commemorations include the anniversaries of Trafalgar, the Victoria Cross, and the Abolition of the slave trade

The working day continues into the evening. There is a weekly meeting with the Prime Minister, usually on Wednesdays, and at 7.30 a report is delivered on the day's parliamentary proceedings. At regular intervals there will be official engagements such as a film première, a concert in aid of a charitable cause, or a reception linked to organisations of which she is patron.

As well as official engagements the Queen's diary is frequently dominated by tours. Her Majesty has made more than 250 visits to over 130 countries.

In the spring of her Diamond Wedding Anniversary year she made a state visit to the USA, exactly 50 years since her first tour. Accompanied by the Duke of Edinburgh, she revisited Jamestown, the site of the first permanent English settlement which celebrated its 400th anniversary in 2007.

The Queen's visit was preceded by the release of a series of photographs by American photographer Annie Leibovitz, best known for her depictions of rock stars. The Queen has sat for more than 140 official portraits: most have been commissioned by organisations. A Rolf Harris portrait, for instance, was commissioned by the BBC for her 80th birthday. As is common with royal portraits, two sittings of one hour each were permitted while Harris worked in oils, and he also used photographs for reference in his studio. Towards the end of his endeavour he borrowed the Queen's dress to refine the details. The painting took two months to complete and the resulting documentary was watched by nearly 7 million people. While the Queen never comments on her portraits, she did offer the opinion to Harris that it was "a very friendly painting".

Harris's amiable and informal depiction shows just how far royal portraiture has come in the centuries since Elizabeth I's policy of image control. One of the most recent commissions was by Royal Mail for the Diamond Wedding celebrations. Lord Snowdon photographed the royal couple early in 2007 in the White Drawing Room at Buckingham Palace, scene of countless royal portraits. A photo of them on the balcony was used for a stamp (page 127). The session also produced striking images such as the more formal side profiles of the couple, elegantly dressed in blue, lit by the open window to which they gaze.

Recent portraits of Her Majesty range from the populist Rolf Harris painting to Snowdon's elegant profiles of the royal couple for their diamond wedding anniversary

DIAMOND LIFE

During the six decades of their married life, the Queen and the Duke of Edinburgh have witnessed enormous change. Since the austerity years following the Second World War the country has seen tremendous regeneration of the inner cities, new building on an unprecedented scale, the replacement of traditional industries by new technologies and services, and increasing national prosperity. The royal family became the first to be exposed to the full glare of the media and life

in the public spotlight. And while this has been uncomfortable at times, the institution of the monarchy remains an important and respected part of national life with the Queen's popularity undiminished.

The Queen and the Duke of Edinburgh celebrated their diamond wedding in November 2007: the first ever such anniversary by a reigning monarch. This was marked by an

issue of six stamps, designed by David Hillman and showing the Queen and Prince Philip smiling as they take part in a variety of official engagements. The first stamp captures them in 1947, at the launch of liner *Caronia*, the last official engagement before their marriage.

In addition to this sequence of portraits of the couple was an eye-catching mini sheet bearing four stamps in the style of a photo album, with more informal photos charting family celebrations. One features the royal family at the 25th wedding anniversary at Balmoral in 1972, while the earliest, from 1951 and also at Balmoral, shows the royal couple with the young Prince Charles and Princess Anne. The most recent picture is by Lord Snowdon and was a special commission by Royal Mail for the diamond wedding anniversary – the royal couple depicted in Buckingham Palace early in 2007, looking at each other on a balcony.

Stamps featuring the Queen are almost always the most popular issued by Royal Mail, and the informality of the more recent issues underlines the changes in how we expect to see contemporary monarchy depicted.

Despite the more relaxed approach in its depiction, the monarchy remains a source of fascination; royal figures are familiar to us, but also remote. They are a focus for elaborate ceremonial and are the embodiment of the state. Perhaps we value the monarchy so much because it is so unlike everything else in our lives. In a recent public poll, 70 per cent of the public was in favour of the monarchy. The same poll asked people what interested them the most. Out of a range of options, top of the list was the royal family, ahead of cartoon family The Simpsons and celebrity couples. In the line that stretches from William the Conqueror to the 40th British monarch, our Queen, it seems clear that the continuum of the monarchy remains highly prized – it is one constancy in our changing times.

The miniature sheet features four stamps, deliberately angled to echo a collection of family photos: three family portraits and one taken in 2007 by Snowdon as part of the Royal Mail commission

All photographs are copyright Royal Mail Group Ltd
except the following:

p.7 The Mall Galleries; p.14 Hulton Archive; p.15 (top)
Hulton Archive; p.15 (below) Souvenir coronation
programmes, The British Library; p.18 (top) photograph
by Cecil Beaton / Camera Press; p.18 (below) both BL;
p.19 (below right) The National Portrait Gallery;
pp 20-21 BL; p.25 photograph by Lord Snowdon / Camera
Press; p.35 Hulton Archive; p.36 photograph by Cecil
Beaton / Victoria & Albert Museum; p.37 (left) BL;
p.37 (right) National Portrait Gallery; p.40 Crown
Copyright; p.48 (bottom right) and p.49 De La Rue Global
Services; p.52 (bottom left) BL; p.53 (main picture)
Mirrorpix.com; p.53 (inset) BL; p.55 (left) BL; p.56 Hulton
Archive; p.57 (left) Tim Graham Picture Library; p.65 both
BL; p.67 BL; p.71 (left) all three BL; p.81 (left) Tim Graham
Picture Library; p.81 (right) BL; p.82 (top) BL; p.84 (left)
photograph by Lord Snowdon; p.84 (right) BL;
p.88 photograph by Barry Hollis / Kent Messenger;
p.99 (main picture) Mirrorpix.com; p.104 all BL;
p.105 National Portrait Gallery; p.106 (top) BL;
p.106 (below) Louisa Buller, Associated Press; p.107
both Hulton Archive; p.112 Rex Features Ltd; p.113 Rex
Features Ltd; p.117 Rex Features Ltd; p.123 Tim
Graham/Getty Images; p.125 Rex Features Ltd (top) and
Photograph by Snowdon, Camera Press London (bottom)

Photographs on pp 4-5, 10-11, 26-27, 44-45, 60-61, 74-75,
92-93 by Dorothy Wilding © Royal Mail Group Ltd
Portraits of artists and studios on pp 38-9, 50, 100 from
'Picture to Post' by GPO Film Unit, courtesy British Postal
Museum and Archive © Royal Mail Group Ltd

BL = The British Library, Philatelic Collections,
Universal Postal Union Collection

This revised and expanded edition published 2007 by

The British Library
96 Euston Road
London NW1 2DB
and
Royal Mail
148 Old Street
London EC1V 9HQ

First published in 2002 in hardback as: *Queen Elizabeth II: A Jubilee Portrait in Stamps*

UK stamp designs copyright © Royal Mail Group Ltd 1952-2008
All other illustrations copyright © The British Library and other
named copyright holders 2007
Text copyright © Royal Mail Group Ltd and The British Library 2007

The Royal Mail cruciform is a registered trademark of Royal Mail Group Ltd

British Library Cataloguing in Publication Data
A catalogue record for this book is available from The British Library

ISBN 978 0 7123 5002 0

Designed and typeset by **Bobby Birchall**
Printed in Hong Kong by **South Sea International Press**
Written by **Fay Sweet**